Small-Boat Cruising to Alaska

Leif G. Terdal

D0062770

HARA
PUBLISHING GROUP

**Published by
Hara Publishing
P.O. Box 19732
Seattle, WA 98109**

Copyright © 2000 by Leif Terdal

All rights reserved

ISBN: 1-883697-04-2

Library of Congress Catalog Card Number:
99-096380

Manufactured in the United States
10 9 8 7 6 5 4 3 2

Editor: Vicki McCown
Cover Design: Scott Fisher
Book Design & Production: Scott & Shirley Fisher

Contents

Acknowledgments

Few boaters travel to Alaska in boats less than 30 feet long. However, trailerable boats that are seaworthy, and have an enclosed cabin with a heater, can be very suitable for extended cruising voyages to Alaska along the Inside Passage. I would like to express my appreciation to Leif Knutsen and his son, Severin, and to Andy and Loris Peace and their daughter, Sherry, for providing in detail their adventures while cruising to Alaska.

The open waters of the Pacific off Northern California, Oregon, Washington and British Columbia present serious challenges, and I wish to thank Peter and Natalie Bates, and Paul Terdal for their insights and perspectives on cruising the open Pacific while en route to and from Alaska. I also wish to thank Ichirou Moriwaki, who traveled from Japan to Glacier Bay across the Pacific in his 26-foot blue-water sailboat on his first major leg of his circumnavigation cruise around the globe. He continues to write me follow-up notes from distant ports.

I am grateful for the assistance provided by Gloria Cranmer Webster and Barbara Boas for sharing their insights and historical knowledge of the struggles of the Kwakiutl Natives and their recent successes in renewing age-old traditions. I also wish to thank Harvey Humchitt, Jack Cabena, and David Boyce for providing information and perspectives about the salmon fisheries and canneries in British Columbia.

I appreciate the help from Ron Marvin, Director of the Interpretive Program of the Tongass Marine Highway, and

Randy Hojem of the U.S. Forest Service for providing a historical background of the great Tongass National Forest and its management.

I am grateful for Chuck Root, Rev. Fritz Youra, Warren Fay, Donald Nelson, John Keiter, Paul and Emily Keller, and especially my wife, Marjorie Terdal, for reading the manuscript in its various stages and providing valuable suggestions.

My special thanks go to the editor, Vicki McCown, and Scott and Shirley Fisher for their invaluable assistance on the text and production.

Introduction

I firmly believe for every ten persons who actually make a trip up the Inside Passage to Alaska, another hundred dream of doing it. The Inside Passage is remarkable in terms of its beauty, its history, and its suitability for passage by serious boaters—even with modest boats. This book is about traveling to S.E. Alaska by private boat through the Inside Passage—and along the outside—in small boats, showing that it can be done safely and with great enjoyment.

Aside from enjoying the spectacular scenery and opportunities to view wildlife, a visitor can learn much about the history of British Columbia and S.E. Alaska by visiting the large canneries (now abandoned), commercial fishing villages, sites of massive logging harvests, and remnants of the gold rush. Opportunities to learn about the cultural history of Native Indians in British Columbia and in Alaska is readily available by viewing totem poles and ancient petroglyphs that remain where they were first created—in the case of petroglyphs as long as 10,000 years ago. Information about Native culture and history is available in Native cultural centers in Alert Bay, B.C., and in Hoonah, Kake, and Angoon in S.E. Alaska, as well as in museums in Juneau, Ketchikan, Petersburg, Wrangell, Sitka, and Skagway.

There are two ways to travel to S.E. Alaska—by water or by air. Auto travel is not a good option because no roads connect cities in S.E. Alaska, and the attractive remote areas such as Glacier Bay National Park and Misty Fjord National Monument are without roads. Air travel has the advantage of speed, but travelers miss the beauty of the magnificent marine environment. Cruising north to S.E. Alaska via British Columbia by boat is the best way.

Travel by cruise ships is extremely popular, with over 500,000 passengers reaching S.E. Alaska by that means alone in 1997, with the expectation that the numbers will increase. The number of people who travel the Inside Passage to Alaska by private boat cannot compare. The contrast can best be seen in Ketchikan when cruise ships arrive and unload passengers, their vast numbers dwarfing the residents of the town and even more so the boaters who arrive with their own vessels.

Pros and Cons of Cruise Ship Travel Versus Independent Boat Travel

There are vast differences in the experiences, cost, and time involved between travel by cruise ship versus private boat. The experiences retained in memory are certainly different. This has been pointed out to me in numerous conversations with those who have returned from cruise ship travel. While most speak highly of the trip and their enjoyment of wondrous scenery and remarkable chances to view wildlife, their memory for places is quite different than that of independent boaters. Those operating their own vessels must review navigational charts, plot a course, measure its distance, estimate running time, and keep a log. They also must keep in mind options to change plans when the conditions warrant. All this requires much more planning and organization than is necessary for those who take a cruise. This mental activity not only adds enjoyment and risk appraisal, but also reinforces memory of places and scenic wonders encountered along the way. As an example, all boaters who navigate Seymour Narrows must be aware of its potential hazard and know how to plan for a safe passage. I have not met one cruise ship passenger who had any memory of this dramatic place or any appreciation of its significance. The same is true for such places along the Canadian Inside Passage, such as historic—and now abandoned—canneries, Namu and Butedale, or the Native villages of New Bella Bella and Klemtu.

Other differences between traveling by private boat versus cruise ship are time and money. Most recreational boaters traveling the Inside Passage from the Puget Sound area to Alaska plan on a two-month trip, whereas cruise ship travel typically lasts one week. The time difference is not due to the speed of the vessels, but the operation, as cruise ships will travel 24 hours a day on certain legs of the trip. Recreational boaters don't do this, but will allow time to explore remote places and small anchorages in coves and other places inaccessible via cruise ships.

Cost is another difference. Traveling by private boat is generally more expensive than by a cruise ship because of the expense of vessel ownership, including depreciation, operating and maintenance costs, insurance and moorage fees. There are also special costs for navigating the Inside Passage. Navigational charts to cover the distance cost as much as $1,500 but can be reused on subsequent trips, and the resale value is very high. Dinghies are necessary because anchoring and rowing to shore is more common in Alaskan waters than tying up to a dock. Fuel and moorage expenses on a trip to Alaska are probably not as high as most people think. For example, fuel costs for a round trip from Port Townsend, Washington, to Glacier Bay National Park in Alaska will range from $750 for a boat with a single diesel engine to $6,000 for a cruiser with twin gasoline engines.

Who travels to Alaska and in what kinds of boats? In July, 1995, in the harbor at Victoria, B.C., I had a chance to view the magnificant yacht Itaska and to speak with some of the crew. The Itaska is a 175-foot, 920-ton, Dutch-built trawler converted to a private yacht and owned by William Simon, a former cabinet member during the Nixon presidency. In the summer of 1994, the Itaska made a successful voyage of the Northwest Passage from Nome, Alaska, traversing Canada and concluding in Greenland. This trip was first accomplished by the Norwegian explorer Roald Amundsen in 1906.

In 1996, in Klemtu, B.C., I saw a beautiful and well-constructed dugout canoe made from a large cedar tree by Natives who told me of their plans to paddle to Victoria and then on to Neah Bay, Washington, to commemorate a traditional and historic voyage. The canoe took seven men one full year to build with hand tools. For tens of generations, similar Native-built canoes were used to travel in Alaskan waters and throughout British Columbia and Washington State.

The contrast in boats was considerable—a most modern yacht as compared with a canoe built to ancient dimensions and form. But for both there was the pursuit of adventure, travel, respect for the environment and a realistic appraisal of risk that brings caution but not resignation to staying at home.

Boaters who travel to Alaska on their own boats use more common fare. I checked with the manager of the Prince Rupert Yacht Club, who reviewed his log of vessels on their way to Alaska from the U.S. and from other countries. Of 42 boats that entered his marina in May 1996 (whose owners stipulated Alaska as their designation), 28 were 40 feet long or longer. Only three vessels were less than 30 feet.

More than one-half came from the state of Washington. About a third were sailboats, some from as far away as Australia.

Why Focus on Small-Boat Cruising to Alaska?

If I had a choice of size and type of boat to cruise the Inside Passage to Alaska, I would choose a trawler about 36 to 42 feet long, with a cruising speed of about ten knots. The choice would be based on the comfort that larger boats offer in terms of space and amenities. Instead, I purchased a small diesel-powered cruiser of just 26 feet, with a cruising speed of 16 knots. It may seem absurd, but my choice of a relatively small boat was based on safety. I wanted to avoid the risks associated with cruising the ocean waters off the Oregon and Washington coast. My choice was based in large part on the fact that I do not live in the state of Washington, and it is difficult for a nonresident to moor a boat in that state. Not only was it inconvenient to check on a boat moored out of state, but Washington places a substantial property tax on nonresidents who moor their boats on a permanent basis in their state. For serious boaters who do not have access to moorage in Puget Sound, they have a problem getting their boat to a starting point to begin their journey up the Inside Passage.

The Question of Acceptable Risk

The question of acceptable risk for a boater going north to Alaska can be put as follows: Given the sea and weather conditions that are likely to be encountered, can you and your vessel handle them safely? For traveling up the Oregon and Washington coastline (the Outside Passage), that question can be restated as follows: Can you and your vessel tolerate winds of 25 to 30 knots with steep six- to eight-foot waves for 24 or more hours before entering a port?

I have encountered those conditions twice while traveling north from the mouth of the Columbia River and on to La Push, Washington, and from La Push around Cape Flattery and into the Strait of Juan de Fuca. I have spoken with scores of boaters who have traveled (or attempted to travel) the Outside Passage up the California, Oregon, and Washington coast. One man from San Francisco made five attempts to leave his home port to head up the northern California coast on his way to Alaska. After being beaten back by strong winds over and over, he arranged to have his large trawler trucked from San Francisco to Anacortes, Washington. I spoke with another man who was so exhausted by his effort to sail his 42-foot sailboat from Coos Bay, Oregon, to Alaska that, after reaching Puget Sound, he decided to end his trip and return home. He mentioned that during one 12-hour period, he made less than six miles of progress while heading into steep waves driven by northwest winds that exceeded 30 knots. He stayed at sea during the bad weather because of the dangers associated with crossing the hazardous bars along the Oregon and Washington Coast.

For the reasons stated above, a boater living outside of the Puget Sound area would do well to consider towing his boat to Anacortes or some other place within Puget Sound, rather than make an open voyage up the Oregon or Washington coast. If towing a boat becomes a serious consideration, then a trailerable boat makes sense.

The question of acceptable risk when traveling the Inside Passage from the Puget Sound area to Alaska is considerably different from the appraisal stated above for the open-ocean voyage. Acceptable risk can be assessed by asking the following: "Can you and your vessel safely handle a change of weather and sea conditions including winds of 25 to 30 knots and steep waves of three to four feet for one to two hours before you can enter a place of safety such as a wind-sheltered cove or protected anchorage?" Although I don't minimize the risk that may be encountered while cruising the Inside Passage, the level of risk is considerably different and less than what one is likely to endure in extended open-ocean cruising.

I was very interested in obtaining information from boaters who had successfully completed the Inside Passage cruise to Alaska and back to review their experiences based on different hull and engine configurations and sail versus power boats. I know there is no perfect boat that suits all. But by talking to boaters in some detail about their extended cruise ships, it became very clear to me that, once a boater has clarified for himself what he wishes to accomplish and over what time frame, there are clear choices to be made among boats, such as sailboats versus power boats, power boats with planing hulls versus displacement hulls, and different engine options. While there is not one "perfect" boat, there can be a good match between a boater's purpose and goal in boating and a particular boat.

The next chapter reviews personal accounts of the experiences of five boaters who traveled the distance between a port in Puget Sound to Alaska. Three made the trip in power boats and two in sailboats. For comparison purposes, I have included summary information from a cruise ship that regularly cruises the Canadian and Alaskan Inside Passage. I have scripted the journeys into legs of the trip to Alaska, with three legs within British Columbia and the fourth from

Prince Rupert to Ketchikan. Leg one (distance approximately 160 miles) covers the distance from ports in the Puget Sound area leading to and including the length of the Strait of Georgia. Leg number two (108 miles) covers the area between Campbell River, sitting at the northern end of the Strait of Georgia, to Port Hardy at the northern tip of Vancouver Island. This important part of the trip covers beautiful marine waters created by past glacial activity originating from massive ice fields in the very high mountains of British Columbia. Leg three (270 miles) covers the long distance from Port Hardy to Prince Rupert, B.C. This leg covers one open-ocean passage across Queen Charlotte Sound and from that point goes through a very remote, roadless, sparsely populated and beautiful portion of British Columbia. This section of the trip requires a boater to be fully prepared with fuel and provisions. Leg four (90 miles) covers the area from Prince Rupert to Ketchikan, and includes an open-ocean section known as the Dixon Entrance. Essentially all boaters traveling to Alaska via the Inside Passage follow this route. This makes it especially useful to compare experiences of boaters going through the same waters. Once a boater arrives in Ketchikan, there are many options for further cruising in Alaskan waters.

Six Boats, One Passage

This chapter reviews the boating experiences of five boater families who successfully cruised the Inside Passage from Puget Sound to Alaska. Accounts of these trips permit one to consider how choices in various types of boats can be made to provide a good match with purpose and expectations of such a trip, as well as constraints. Three boaters cruised to Alaska with small (less than 30 feet) trailerable boats, and two others "motored" up with comfortable sailboats. The first account of a trip taken by Leif Knutsen and son is given in some detail to provide an overview of the Inside Passage through British Columbia to Ketchikan. To avoid repetition (since the route is essentially the same for all who cruise the passage), less day-to-day detail is given in the other accounts. An important exception is made concerning the two routes from the end of the Strait of Georgia to the Queen Charlotte Strait. The passage that is the alternative to that taken by Leif Knutsen is also described.

This chapter also contains perspectives of most interesting highlights shared by three of the families. Highlights experienced by the other two are included in a subsequent chapter on cruising the Outside Passage to Alaska and in my account of cruising the Canadian and Alaskan Inside Passages. Included also are summary tables that review fuel consumption, average distance traveled per day by the boaters, and speed of travel. This information is not to portray that a cruise to Alaska is like a race, but to give a realistic appraisal of the time one should plan to set aside. Finally, I have included information from a cruise ship (Sky

Princess) concerning information about the phase of its trip from Vancouver, B.C., to Ketchikan, Alaska.

Leif Knutsen and 13-year-old son, Severin
Port Townsend, Washington, to Glacier Bay area, Alaska
Vessel: Shadow Fay
(powered by one ten-horsepower outboard)

The following account of a cruise up the Inside Passage to Alaska, from Port Townsend, Washington, by Leif Knutsen and his son is of interest for several reasons. They made the trip with an owner-designed and-built vessel powered by one ten-horsepower outboard engine. I was intrigued because, in my native Norway, a number of boaters explore the Norwegian coastline in boats about 26 feet in length and powered by a single-cylinder diesel engine of about nine horsepower. The boat built by Leif Knutsen is the only one with such low horsepower I know of in the States that was designed and built for serious long-range cruising. He provides clear evidence that it is feasible to travel the Inside Passage in a well-built but small boat. He took maximum advantage of tidal currents, so that while his boat traveled over water at about five knots, he frequently averaged seven or eight knots when measured in speed over ground. When the currents were against him, he pulled into an anchorage or cove and waited for the tide to turn. When the tidal currents were in his favor, he traveled on without regard to the time of day or night. Another point of interest is his view of beauty, danger and time, which he explains in his narrative.

Leif Knutsen

I am a shipwright and part owner of the Port Townsend Co-op, where we work on ship construction and repair. My vessel, the Shadow Fay, is a 25-foot inshore fisheries and utilities boat. I designed and built the vessel, with design assistance from a marine architect from Vancouver Island. The hull is a computer (Ship Cam) redesign of the proven Chincoteague fishing skiff described in *American Small Sailing Craft* by Howard I. Chapelle.

The 25-foot, all-welded aluminum vessel meets all current and proposed United States Coast Guard regulations applicable to commercial vessels of less than 50 feet. She also meets current federal regulations for charter vessels carrying six passengers or less.

Propulsion is provided via a ten-horsepower Yamaha high-thrust four-cycle outboard on a sliding transom in a deep well. Auxiliary power for the boat is supplied with a 185-square-foot roller-furling headsail for beam reach or downwind conditions.

Our vessel was designed as a commercial inshore fisheries boat, with a fish hold capacity of 1800 pounds. This was a test run for the boat, and my son and I had no intention of—nor were we set up for—commercial fishing. The point of our test run was to demonstrate that one can take an extended cruise at hull speed (about five knots per hour) in a seaworthy boat with a low-horsepower engine and at outstanding fuel economy. This would be my twelfth trip to Alaska by boat; all the other trips were on large commercial fishing boats. I also wanted to demonstrate that it was possible to build a low-cost fishing vessel that is within the financial reach of many owner-operator commercial fishermen. The boat can also be modified

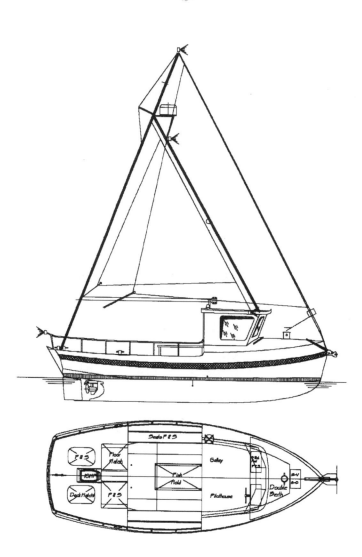

Leif Knutsen's Shadow Fay, a 25-foot Inshore Fisherman

and built as a "mom and pop" cruiser with a much larger cabin area.

Leg I:
Port Townsend, Washington, to Campbell River, B.C.

This part of our journey took us across the Strait of Juan de Fuca, then on north through the Canadian Gulf Islands, where we entered the Strait of Georgia outside of Nanaimo.

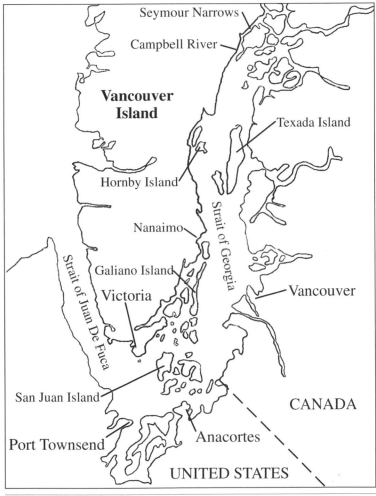

From there we proceeded up the Strait of Georgia to Campbell River.

July 18, 1994

We left Port Townsend at 2 a.m. in order to catch the last of the dying ebb. This assisted us as we proceeded northwest. After passing Smith Island (halfway across the Strait), the current turned to flood and again helped us as we proceeded north. Continuing on the Canadian side of San Juan Island, we followed a route staying east of Saltspring Island and along the Trincomali Channel, which is bordered on the east side by Galiano Island. We pulled in on the south side of Secretary Island that night and anchored.

We left early the next morning, followed the Stuart Channel, crossed the Dodd Narrows, and entered Nanaimo where we stopped briefly for fuel and supplies. From Nanaimo we crossed into the Strait of Georgia. The winds were calm and we continued on, stopping at Ford Cove on the southwest side of Hornby Island at 5:45 p.m., taking on some more fuel and supplies. We continued on and arrived at Campbell River at 2 a.m. on the 20th. We stopped for about two hours at the government dock to rest briefly and to time our approach to Seymour Narrows.

Leg II:
Campbell River to Port Alexander (Port Hardy area)

This part of our journey took us into Discovery Passage at the northwest end of the Strait of Georgia. From there we proceeded past Seymour Narrows and continued on until we reached Johnstone Strait. We followed Johnstone Strait, which is open to northwest winds, and continued on until

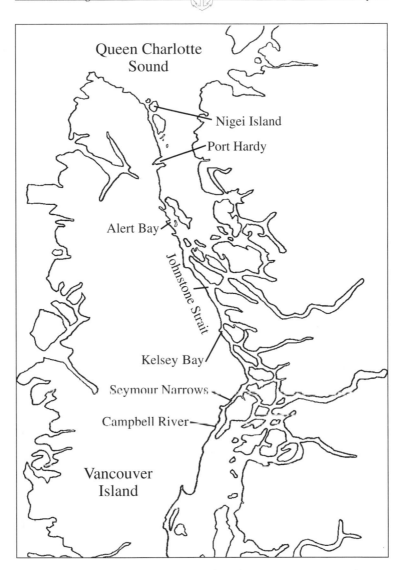

we entered Queen Charlotte Strait, where our goal was to anchor at Port Alexander on the southeast side of Nigei Island.

July 20, 1994

We left on the 20th before dawn (4 a.m.) and passed through the Seymour Narrows just after high tide and with the current again in our favor. We entered Brown Bay to pick up more fuel and ice, then continued on up Discovery Passage. We pulled into Otter Cove, below Chatham Point, at 11 a.m., anchored and got some much-needed rest. Stopping was to our advantage because a big flood tide was coming in with a strong current against us.

We left Otter Cove at 1 p.m., made the turn at Chatham Point and stayed close to shore on the southern side of Johnstone Strait to work the back eddies. The tide did turn and an interesting thing happened just outside of West Thurlow Island. We stayed on the southern edge of Johnstone Strait and the water was calm. But not far from us, in an area called Ripple Shoal, there was white water with standing waves about four feet high. The currents pouring through the many large inlets caused the rough-water conditions. We saw the turbulence ahead of us, but for a while we remained out of it and enjoyed a quiet ride. Finally, we moved into the area of choppy water with white caps. I don't remember any time going through Johnstone Strait without some rough water. Wind often comes through the area in the afternoon and it can get nasty. We continued on and pulled into Kelsey Bay at 5:30 p.m. We had covered a lot of territory in three days, but we were hustling to go north.

We left Kelsey Bay at 4:45 a.m. on the 21st and arrived at Alert Bay (a distance of 40 nautical miles) that morning at 9:15 a.m. We fueled up, got some good ice and walked around the dock. Later we walked to the southern part of the town and saw the totem poles and the Native cemetery.

We left Alert Bay at 1:15 p.m. and pulled into Port Alexander on the southeast end of Nigei Island. We had, in just a few days, completed one-half of the journey through the Canadian Inside Passage. When conditions were favorable, we crossed the open waters of Queen Charlotte Sound.

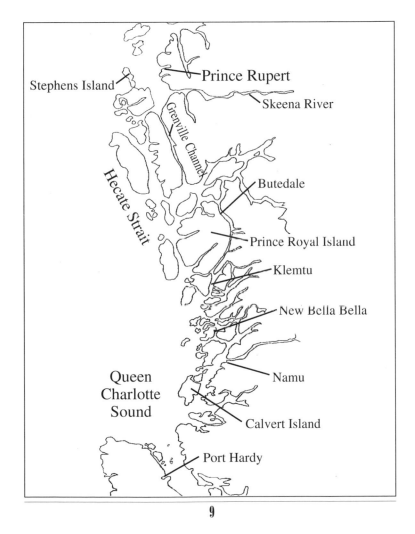

Leg III:
Port Alexander (Port Hardy area) to Prince Rupert

This part of our journey took us across Queen Charlotte Sound past Cape Caution. The open ocean section of this passage (from Pine Island to the southern tip of Calvert Island) is about 35 miles. From there we proceeded north through very protected waters to Prince Rupert.

July 22, 1994

We left Port Alexander at 5 a.m. under calm conditions but during an ebb tide, ignoring the standard advice: "Never cross Queen Charlotte Sound during an ebb tide." That advice is true if there is a northwest wind and rough seas. But we were lucky and the seas were very quiet, so we took advantage of the ebb tide, which gave us more speed over ground. After leaving Port Alexander, we went through Browning Passage and hit open water. This is referred to as the Outside Passage. We took a path west of Pine Island, then past Storm Islands, and proceeded north on the west side of Egg Island. After a pleasant and uneventful trip across the open water, we entered Fitz Hugh Sound just east of Calvert Island.

Time, Beauty and Danger

I have a theory about time as it pertains to beauty and danger. I like to take the time to appreciate beauty. I prefer to walk through beauty slowly. I'm always amazed when tourists drive up to a major scenic point or national monument, get out of their car, take a picture, and go on. That is not for me. Also, to make a thing seem even bigger, it is important to spend time. Think of the difference between one who says "I saw a bear" as compared to one who says "I spent three hours viewing a bear feeding on salmon in a stream." Wildlife viewing is different from a momentary glance or brief sighting. It helps to learn about what you have seen or expect to see, to read about the experiences you may encounter, and to get information from museums or other sources. All of this takes time but makes the experiences more memorable.

I believe the same thing holds true when danger is encountered. Preparation takes time but helps make a dangerous situation more understandable and manageable. If one encounters hazardous sea conditions, for example, the person is better off having established a habit of performing some basic tasks: reviewing navigational charts, keeping track of position, reviewing instrument readings on the vessel, and paying attention to the sea conditions at hand. All of this takes time. This is my thought about the connection between time, beauty and danger: Beauty is vastly more appreciated if a person takes the time and effort to learn and to observe and not just be content with a fleeting glance. Similarly, a dangerous situation is much more manageable if a person takes the time to learn, to anticipate, to respond thoughtfully, and to review when the passage "event" is over.

On this trip, Severin and I were passing through a beautiful but unprotected area of open sea. Our speed of just over five knots let us take the beauty in. If we would have encountered rough conditions, this major passage would have seemed even bigger—but we were prepared.

We continued cruising north in Fitz Hugh Sound until we pulled into Namu Harbor at 2:30 p.m. Namu Harbor was once an active salmon cannery, of which there were large numbers in British Columbia. Now most are defunct and abandoned. When we stopped at Namu in 1994, there was a store stocked with food, but no one was in it or around it. I found a lone caretaker who was willing to sell me fuel. We departed Namu at 4:45 p.m., proceeded up Fisher Channel, made a turn at Kaiete Point into Lama Passage, and anchored for the night about three miles below New Bella Bella at 8:30 p.m. The whole trip so far had gone very well. We were now in a wilderness setting, with beautiful channels and inlets and numerous bald eagles. We frequently saw salmon jumping out of the water. Severin commented that it was like a *Bambi* movie.

July 23, 1994

We left at 5:30 a.m. and headed up the line. We bypassed New Bella Bella and arrived at Ivory Island at 8:15 a.m. and decided to go through Reid Passage to avoid Milbanke Sound. At 1:10 p.m. we were at the west end of Jackson Passage and into Finlayson Channel. We bypassed Klemtu, a Native fishing village, and proceeded north. At the end of Jane Island we turned west and entered Tolmie Channel, which is bordered by Sarah Island on the east and Princess Royal Island on the west.

We continued up Tolmie Channel and anchored at Butedale at 10 p.m. Butedale was once a major salmon cannery and fish processing plant but was abandoned sometime in the late 1960s or early 1970s. We spoke with a couple of men who are trying to make a go of the area—not as a cannery but as a supply and moorage stopover for commercial and recreational boaters traveling the Inside Passage. As Severin and I prepared a late dinner, we reviewed the day and realized that on this day, the 23rd of July, we covered 86 nautical miles in 17 hours, and we did so in the presence of magnificent scenery.

July 24, 1994

We left Butedale at 6 a.m. and proceeded up Fraser Reach, turned west at Kingcome Point, and entered McKay Reach. We then crossed Wright Sound and were about to head into Grenville Channel. I was concerned about my fuel supply because we had last fueled up at Namu. While still in Wright Sound, we took a side trip to Hartley Bay, which is a small First Nation (Native) village, to buy some fuel. Hartley Bay does have a government dock for transient moorage, but no fuel dock. I was able to buy eight gallons of gasoline from the personal stock of a resident fisherman of Hartley Bay. We left Hartley Bay after our short stop, proceeded south a few miles, and entered Grenville Channel. The weather was sunny, warm (low 60s), and the waters were calm. We also had an incoming tide, going in our direction, as we proceeded up the channel towards the Prince Rupert area; the tidal current increased our speed over ground by about two knots. We continued up Grenville Channel into the evening under beautiful conditions. We bypassed Lowe Inlet which is a favorite anchorage of mine and pulled into Ship Anchorage (about ten miles further up the Channel) to anchor for the night.

July 25, 1994

We pulled anchor at 5 a.m. and moved up the channel, arriving at the Native town of Metlakatla at 3:40 p.m. We

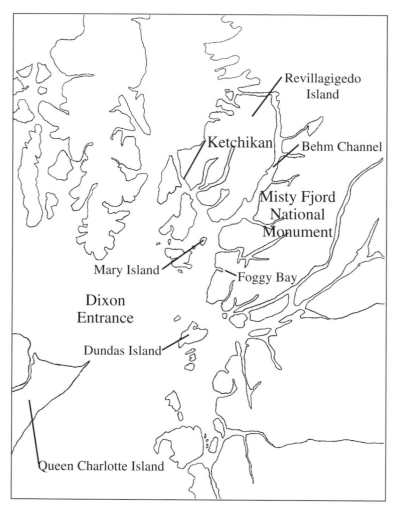

were now just about 85 nautical miles from Ketchikan. We fueled up at Metlakatla and did not make the short side trip (six miles) to Prince Rupert via the Venn Passage.

Leg IV:
Prince Rupert area (Metlakatla) to Ketchikan, Alaska

This part of our journey takes us across the Dixon Entrance and the international border (at latitude 54.40) into Alaskan waters.

July 26, 1994

We left Metlakatla at 7 a.m. and headed on out across the Dixon Entrance. As we left, there were showers, a light breeze from the southeast and calm seas. Still this portion of the trip along the Inside Passage represents a major hurdle. Had the seas been rough we would have waited until things settled down. We crossed the Alaskan-Canadian line at about 11:20 a.m. Two hours later we were outside of Tree Point Light. From there we went on up to Foggy Bay and entered Very Inlet at 5 p.m. where we anchored. It was now raining hard. We had crossed into Foggy Bay when the tide was slack. This is important because a tidal waterfall forms in a section of this area during maximum current flows. The turbulence is created by the tremendous flow of water through narrow passages when up to a 23-foot vertical change in tide occurs in just a six-hour period. The anchorage itself is reached from the north through a passage that is narrow and deep. The best anchorage is in the east portion.

July 27, 1994

We took off at 11 a.m. to catch slack water and the beginning of an ebb. We arrived in Ketchikan at 6 p.m this evening. I had called customs from my boat before arriving in Ketchikan; however, they would close before we could get there, so I arranged to check in with them the next morning.

Remainder of trip:

Severin and I continued to explore Alaskan waters. We were most interested in exploring coves and inlets and out-of-the-way anchorages, not the cities. We visited Thorne Bay on the Prince of Wales Island and small cities such as Wrangell and Petersburg. Cruising to Juneau, we visited with friends and from there went around Mansfield Peninsula (northern part of Admiralty Island) and into Icy Strait before returning home to Port Townsend, Washington.

Favorite area: Anan Creek Bear Observatory

One of my very favorite spots is the Anan Creek Bear Observatory about 30 miles south of Wrangell. Anan Creek, which drains Anan Lake into a bay, has one of the largest runs of pink salmon in S.E. Alaska. There is a forest service trail that leads to a bear observatory. The observatory itself is a platform that overlooks a small waterfall on Anan Creek. Severin and I walked that trail and photographed some of the big black bears feeding on the salmon. We observed until late one evening, returned to our boat to overnight, and visited the bear observatory again the next morning where we spent most of the day. The creek was thick with salmon, and the area had many feeding bears. Many bald eagles were also feeding on the salmon. This is truly what Southeast Alaska is all about!

Summary of trip by Leif Knutsen and Severin
(Port Townsend, Washington, to Ketchikan, Alaska)

Nautical Miles	635
Duration of trip	8 days
Engine hours	115
Average cruising hours per day	14.4
Average distance covered per day	79 miles
Total fuel consumption	60 gallons

Andy and Loris Peace
Anacortes, Washington, to Skagway, Alaska
Vessel: Ginger Kay
(1976 Starcraft Aluminum 25-foot cruiser)

The account of the Inside Passage trip to Alaska by Andy and Loris Peace is of special interest for several reasons. First, this couple made a decision that, considering where they lived (in Caldwell, Idaho), they could best cruise to Alaska in a trailerable boat. There would have been no practical way for them to have owned a very large boat in Idaho and moved it to where they could have cruised the Inside Passage to Alaska. In contrast to the account by Leif Knutsen (described above), Andy and Loris chose a boat with a planing hull and a fast cruising speed. Another point of interest in their account is that Loris Peace has a chronic illness, and still she was eager to make this trip with her husband. Decisions about health and whether or not to seek adventure through travel are concerns all of us may face in time. It is very possible too many of us turn down opportunities because we believe we may be a burden to others, we may face architectural barriers, or we may meet scorn. The travel to Alaska by Andy and Loris Peace can be viewed as "acceptable risk," not careless risk.

Loris Speaks:

In the summer of 1995, my husband approached me with the thought of going to Alaska via the Inside Passage. We owned a sailboat and had experience sailing in the San Juan Islands in Washington State and the Gulf Islands in Canada, as well as the waters in the Strait of Georgia and on up the east coast of Vancouver Island in the waters known as Johnstone Strait and Queen Charlotte Sound.

We did not wish to sail to Alaska because we were interested in a boat that had speed so we could limit travel time to between two to six hours a day. Andy purchased a 1976 Starcraft Aluminum 25-foot cruiser powered by a 351 Windsor V8 and a "kicker" 25-horsepower Evinrude outboard. In preparing for the trip, because our boat is old, Andy replaced all bolts on parts that could not be replaced on the water. We carried a lot of extra parts, including a starter motor, alternator, coil, plugs, carburetor kit, points, rotor cap, solenoid and some wiring. Andy also installed a large fuel filter and water separator to assure clean fuel to the engine. Our boat, named the Ginger Kay after our two granddaughters, has a top speed of approximately 30 knots and a cruising speed of 16 to 22 knots.

Health Concerns

I am a diabetic, legally blind and unable to walk any distance without resting. I had to pack enough insulin and an emergency kit in case my blood sugar fell too low. I also took herbs to keep us well. While walking is difficult for me, it is important for anyone with diabetes to get exercise, to eat well and not to skip any meals. Since a small boat is confining and does not lend itself to exercise, we wanted a fairly fast boat to make some distance and limit travel time.

Leg I:
Anacortes, Washington, to Refuge Cove, B.C.
(Desolation Sound)

We left Anacortes, Washington, the morning of May 21, 1996, and headed west in a direction that took us north of San Juan Island. We arrived at South Pender Island two and a half hours later and checked in at the Canadian Customs Port of Entry. A short time later, we went on to Ganges Harbor on Saltspring Island and stayed there for a couple of days. Andy enjoyed what he described as world-class French pastries, available at Ganges Harbor, but I had to watch my diet.

On the 24th of May, we left Ganges Harbor and followed a route along the Trincomali Channel, just west of Galiano Island, and continued up the Pylades Channel. We exited these very protected waters at Gabriola Passage and entered the Strait of Georgia. The waters were reasonably calm so we made very good time as we crossed over to the mainland side of the Strait of Georgia. We fueled up at the

Westview Boat Harbor just outside of Powell River and continued on to Refuge Cove on West Redonda Island where we moored for the night.

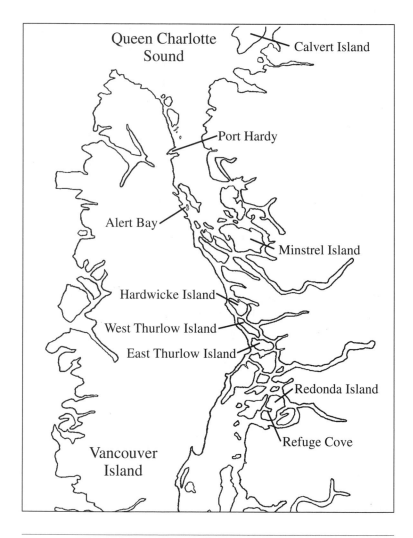

Leg II:
Refuge Cove to Port Hardy

We had a choice between two routes to proceed from the north end of Georgia Strait up to Port Hardy at the northern tip of Vancouver Island. We could have gone by way of Campbell River, then through Discovery Passage, going past Seymour Narrows, and on up to Chatham Point, where we would enter Johnstone Strait. While this is the more direct route, it has more commercial traffic, strong tidal currents and is exposed to potentially strong winds throughout the entire length of Johnstone Strait. We chose the longer route that is referred to as the northern passage to Queen Charlotte Strait from the northern portion of the Strait of Georgia. This latter route meanders around a series of islands which provide buffers against strong winds.

We left Refuge Cove in midmorning on the 26th and stopped briefly at Stuart Island about an hour later, then continued on to Blind Channel Resort on West Thurlow Island. This is a very complete marina and resort, with an excellent restaurant and store that is open year-round. We purchased fuel and left after a short stay, crossing over a narrow channel (Mayne Passage) and anchoring within Charles Bay, located on the northwest side of East Thurlow Island. We left the next morning and went west past Bessborough Bay (on the mainland) and proceeded along Sunderland Channel following the northwest side of Hardwicke Island. Entering Johnstone Strait just west of the area of Kelsey Bay, we followed Johnstone Strait about thirteen miles and turned into Havannah Channel. From there we cruised along Chatham Channel to Minstrel Island, staying there for the night. The Minstrel Island Resort is also open all year and is fully provisioned to supply a boater with supplies, fuel, and guest moorage along with laundry and shower facilities.

On the 29th the winds settled, so we left early to get a good start before the northwest winds began to blow. We covered the distance between Minstrel Island and Alert Bay in just over three hours. We enjoyed a good breakfast at the hotel near the boat harbor and took the short walk to the Native cemetery and the totem poles. We left Alert Bay at noon and arrived at Port Hardy in just over an hour. The harbor was in very poor condition and I had to be very careful walking from the boat to land because of my very limited vision, even with Andy helping me. Some planks were rotten, some missing, and most were tilted. In short, the moorage was terrible, the worst we encountered on the whole trip. We took a taxi into town because I could not walk the distance. We had lunch and bought supplies. It rained hard that night, but we enjoyed a quiet dinner on our small boat and celebrated the completion of this phase of our trip. The next leg of our trip would be across open water from Port Hardy to the east side of Calvert Island.

Leg III:
Port Hardy, B.C., to Prince Rupert, B.C.

Andy and I knew that the crossing from Port Hardy to Calvert Island is a major passage on the route to Alaska. There is about 40-plus miles of open water through Queen Charlotte Sound before reaching the protection offered by land on both sides of the passage. We were anxious about this part of the trip, but on the morning we planned to leave (May 30), the conditions looked good.

We left Port Hardy at about 7 a.m. and went past God's Pocket, turning to a northwesterly direction after passing the Scarlett Point Lighthouse on Balaklava Island. We continued on staying west of Pine Island and, further north, staying to the west side of Egg Island. We arrived at the area of Safety Cove in about five hours but continued on our way. We fueled up at New Bella Bella, then crossed a channel to the east and pulled into the Shearwater Resort. There we ate lunch, showered, did our laundry and stayed for the night.

The remainder of this long leg of the trip to Prince Rupert went without incident. We crossed Milbanke Sound under calm sea conditions, stopped briefly for fuel at the Native village of Klemtu and continued on. We traveled for just two or three hours a day. We spent one night anchored at Horsefly Cove inside Green Inlet. As we proceeded on our way to Prince Rupert, we pulled into a cove known as East Inlet within Grenville Channel and stayed there for two days and nights. Andy dug some clams, and we enjoyed some good meals on board and spent some very quiet time to read and relax. We left East Inlet on June 5 and headed on to Prince Rupert. It was raining and cool, but Grenville Channel is remarkably protected, so we faced no difficult water conditions. We passed Kennedy Island and were into the outflow of the famous Skeena River. Further on we approached Kaien Island, which is the location for Prince Rupert. We arrived at Prince Rupert, the northernmost coastal city in British Columbia—and a great one—at noon.

Leg IV:
Prince Rupert, B.C., to Ketchikan, Alaska

We were concerned about the passage from Prince Rupert to Ketchikan because we had to pass through the famous Dixon Entrance, which is exposed to the open ocean and potentially serious sea conditions. We left Prince Rupert at 5 a.m. and went through the Venn Passage, which cuts through a channel at the north end of Digby Island; this saves about an hour's run around the island. To our great satisfaction the winds were calm and the seas were quite manageable. We proceeded past Dundas Island and into Alaskan waters. About six hours after leaving Prince Rupert, we arrived in Ketchikan. Andy checked in at customs and went grocery shopping. I stayed on board, and the next three days we took in the sights and sound of wind and rain.

Remainder of the trip:

From Ketchikan we continued north with our relaxed boating cruise in S.E. Alaska, stopping at Meyers Chuck, then on to the historic small cities of Wrangell and Petersburg. Traveling to Juneau and nearby Auke Bay we were joined by our daughter, Sherry, who flew in from Idaho. The three of us took a side trip to Tracy Arm, then on to Lynn Canal and historic Skagway. We travelled on to Sitka on the west coast of Southeast Alaska. From there we headed south and retraced our trip to Anacortes, where Andy trailered the small cruiser back to Caldwell, Idaho. Our boating cruise, which began in late May, concluded successfully in mid-September.

Favorite area: Lynn Canal and Skagway

We left Auke Bay on June 24 and went through Lynn Canal on our way to Skagway. We saw lots of humpback whales and often slowed the boat to look in awe. Here are some thoughts from our daughter, Sherry:

Another high point was the humpback whales. We were in Lynn Canal and Dad saw one blow, so we slowed to watch. We could see its back now and then as its path brought it closer to us. As it came within yards of the boat and surfaced, we could see it was two whales, one smaller than the other. They just lay for a moment with their backs exposed, then submerged and took a course slowly widening the gap between us. Further down the canal we saw one blow, so we slowed the boat but maintained our course. He was close to shore, feeding I suppose. Then we saw another blow, and another. Next I heard one blow behind me. I turned in time to see his back and tail. It was so exciting. There were whales all around us—maybe as many as five. I don't know how long we watched them; it was as though I couldn't see enough. First we'd hear the blow, and it was loud, then we could see the water mist quite high. Then their backs would break the surface and at the last minute their flukes would come completely out of the water and glide back in. They were so graceful.

We arrived in Skagway on the afternoon of the 24th. The town is in a beautiful setting on the waterfront with a river on one side and the whole area surrounded by mountains. Andy and Sherry walked to town; when they returned, the three of us went to the beginning of the famous Chilkoot trail. It was an amazing experience to witness the location of such an important part of Alaskan history. When we returned, a man at the dock gave us five salmon steaks for supper; they were delicious. Many times on our trip we witnessed the generosity of Alaskan residents who truly like to share what they have.

Summary of trip by Andy and Loris Peace
(Anacortes, Washington, to Ketchikan, Alaska)

Nautical Miles	about 635
Duration of trip	18 days
Engine hours	40
Average cruising hours per day	2.2 hours
Average distance covered per day	35 miles
Total fuel consumption	300 gallons

Peter and Natalie Bates,
with daughters Jordan, age four years,
Charlotte, age four weeks, and Natalie's father.
Portland, Oregon, to Glacier Bay National Park
Vessel: Blue Oasis
(35-foot motor sailor)

The account of the boating cruise to Alaska by the Bates family is of special interest for several reasons. First, this couple made a decision that, considering the size of their vessel, they would take their motor sailor across the Columbia river bar and travel north along the outside of the Washington coast before turning into the Strait of Juan de Fuca where they could begin the Inside Passage portion of the trip. To have moved their heavy and large vessel to a port within Puget Sound would have required hoisting the boat to dry dock, removing the mast, and hiring a commercial trucking company to transport their boat.

After navigating the difficult ocean waters off the Washington coast and turning into the Strait of Juan de Fuca, they began the Inside Passage portion of their journey at Port Angeles, Washington, eventually reaching Glacier Bay National Park. Their account punctuates the outstanding difference in sea conditions likely to be encountered off the coast of the Pacific Northwest versus the Inside Passage. In this chapter we will only review the Inside Passage portion of their trip. Their "outside" experience is summarized in a later chapter: "The Outside Cruise to Alaska." A second special aspect of their trip is that they took the occasion of the birth of a daughter to make their dreamed-of trip to Alaska as a way to commemorate the birth. They provide insights about the feasibility of making a long voyage with young children.

Peter Bates:

In mid-May, 1996, we were preparing for the birth of our second child. My wife is an engineer for Intel and was negotiating some time off for maternity leave. To our surprise and great satisfaction, my wife was granted a three-month paid leave. This gave us an opportunity to do something that would be memorable, exciting and fun so we could always look back at the occasion of our baby's birth. We could not go backpacking or sea kayaking, the activities we liked the best. We couldn't really travel to Europe, but we could get a boat and go up the Inside Passage to Alaska, an adventure we had thought about since we first moved to Oregon back in 1973.

I spent a lot of time flying around the Northwest looking at boats and talking to brokers. Natalie and I went to Bellingham and Seattle and on up to Vancouver, B.C. We finally found a boat in Portland that seemed suitable. It was a 35-foot Finnish-built motor sailor, with a relatively large diesel engine (85 horsepower) for a sailboat that size. My father-in-law came out from Annapolis, Maryland, and together we prepared the boat and ourselves for the trip.

Summary of the Inside Passage journey from Port Angeles, Washington, to Ketchikan, Alaska:

Leg I:
Port Angeles, Washington, to Desolation Sound, B.C.

Natalie and I were careful to avoid cruising under difficult weather and sea conditions. We left Port Angeles early in the morning on July 5 and crossed the Strait of Juan de Fuca, then proceeded on to Sidney on Vancouver Island. We reported in to Canadian Customs by phone at the dock and then left the protected marina to anchor instead in a quiet cove tucked into Saltspring Island. The next day we proceeded past Dodd Narrows and anchored in a cove at Newcastle Island near Nanaimo. This area was crowded with boats, but we stayed there for two nights. On the 8th of July we left Newcastle Island and headed across the Strait of Georgia. The weather and sea conditions were calm, so we proceeded on to Powell River, and from there to Pendrell Sound on East Redonda Island. We reached Desolation Sound and could easily have spent a summer enjoying this area but we were eager to proceed north.

Leg II:
Desolation Sound to Port Hardy

We chose to proceed to Port Hardy via the Northern Passage to avoid as much of Johnstone Strait as possible. We had heard of the possibility of strong northwest winds and choppy waters. On July 11, we left Pendrell Sound and headed up to cross Yuculta Rapids, situated between Stuart Island and Sonora Island. We then motored past Dent Rapids. The descriptions of these rapids are terrifying (a portion of Dent Rapids is called Devil's Hole—with standing waves). However, we timed our passage to occur at slack tide so that the waters were calm. We gained confidence from navigating through potentially dangerous waters when the tide and currents were favorable. When we arrived at Port Hardy, the northwest winds were very strong and continued for several days. We stayed in port for four days, waiting patiently for the weather and sea conditions to improve. On July 17, the weather cleared and we crossed Queen Charlotte Sound under beautiful and safe conditions. On most days we traveled about five hours, relaxed, hiked on shore when possible, and entertained ourselves on board. We arrived in Ketchikan, Alaska, on July 23.

Remainder of trip:

Our family extensively explored Southeast Alaska by boat. After checking in with U.S. Customs in Ketchikan, we spent several days exploring by boat the Misty Fjord National Monument, completing the 90-plus-mile loop of the Behm Canal. From there we continued north and stopped in at Meyers Chuck. Proceeding north we stopped at the bear observatory at Anan Creek and viewed the bears, bald eagles and the stream full of salmon. We spent a day and a night at Wrangell; however, since we were most interested in wilderness settings, we sought out remote and uninhabited places. At Le Conte Bay we witnessed the huge amount of icebergs and floating ice chunks that continuously break off the massive Le Conte Glacier. Proceeding north, we anchored in Thomas Bay in front of Baird Glacier. Further on we pulled into Hobart Bay and moored at the public dock at Entrance Island. We then powered up, stopping at Taku Harbor, about 20 miles south of Juneau. When we reached Juneau, we thoroughly enjoyed the numerous hiking trails around the city. We believe that Juneau may have the best hiking trails of any city in the United States. We continued on to Glacier Bay National Park and witnessed the abundant bird and marine life—most notably the humpback whales. We especially enjoyed Reid Glacier. Upon returning to Juneau, we found a buyer for our sailboat, sold it and flew back to Portland, Oregon. We will always remember the vacation we took to celebrate the birth of our second daughter, Charlotte—named for the islands west of Prince Rupert, B.C.

Favorite area: The Misty Fjord National Monument

We took off early on the morning of July 24 and headed south from Ketchikan and entered Behm Canal. It was so beautiful. We were waiting the whole time to see spectacular Alaskan scenery, and here it was. Behm Canal is the water route through the Misty Fjord National Monument. It is gorgeous—like combining Yosemite National Park with an inland sea. We took the opportunity to park the boat and hike, which is what we really wanted to do. Our first landfall was Windstanley Island. This area has a mooring buoy and a hiking trail. As we approached it we saw a mother bear and a cub scampering up the trail that we were going to take. The wildlife was abundant, the scenery gorgeous. We hiked up to the lake at Windstanley and walked around that lake. We went back to our boat and motored up to the next big inlet known as Misty Fjord (Rudyard Bay). We hiked up the trail to Punchbowl Lake, one of the most beautiful mountain lakes we've ever seen. The U.S. Forest Service has placed a skiff at the lake and a cabin. It is in the most wilderness of settings. Big boulders have fallen off high cliffs and created a dam forming the lake. These massive rock falls have occurred many times, enlarging the lake with each new rock fall. Recent falls have brought down with them numerous trees from the mountain cliffs, with sheer walls formed by past massive glacial activity. It was an adventure to take in the beauty. We hiked back and saw this wild and beautiful scenery with dramatic mountain cliffs and gorges. We found warm water from a hot spring and took the longest bath. After this long and remarkable day of hiking, we returned to Rudyard Bay and spent the night.

The next day we left Rudyard Bay and continued on to complete the cruise around Behm Canal, all the time taking in the beauty of the Misty Fjord National Monument. Each mile brought a new adventure. At one point we entered the inlet of the Chickamin River, which has a very large flow of water and glacial silt from a major glacier that has retreated and is no longer a tidewater glacier. We went as far into the inlet as we could and still have water below our keel when the tide turned to low slack. We saw no other boats in the area. Convinced that we were anchored safely, we spent the evening taking in the beauty and then retired for the night.

Infants and young children on an extended cruise
to Alaska—our perspective:

After completing our cruise around Behm Canal, we entered Clarence Strait and headed north to Meyers Chuck.

This neat and well-protected small natural harbor is a lovely place. The key to visiting a place like Meyers Chuck, and other very small, remote villages (population less than one hundred) is to have a young child aboard, a commodity like gold. Children who live in places like Meyers Chuck are tired of seeing adults. At Meyers Chuck there were other young children Jordan's age; when they saw she was eager to play, they had a great time together. She and two other young children played all afternoon and again the next morning until we left for other places.

We also found that Jordan was very content to be aboard our boat for such an extended trip. We ate, slept, and traveled on the boat. While that is confining, she much enjoyed playing with Mom, with me, with Grandfather and her new baby sister. She was not at an age where she needed to get out and explore the world on her own.

We believe it is important to have a child-proof boat. Our boat was very durable. A different boat with fine joinery and breakable objects within reach of a curious child could have presented a problem. Safety, of course, is critical, and we set limits as to where she could go when outside the cabin. We always supervised, and she followed our guidelines.

The brand-new baby was no problem, either. She had no special needs that could not easily be met aboard a boat. She was fed by Mom, and the isolation from other people probably reduced the chances of her getting sick. She was well the entire trip. We put her in a car seat that was comfortable for her, and she enjoyed looking at us and smiling and "talking." In our opinion there is no reason not to take an infant—or a young child—to Alaska by boat. We did meet some boaters with children between six and 12 years of age who felt that "child management" was a problem. While I am sure that individual circumstances will override general guidelines, children who are old enough to want some freedom from parental presence—but not yet old enough to appreciate the pristine wilderness of Southeast Alaska—can become testy.

Summary of Trip by the Bates family:
(Port Angeles, Washington, to Ketchikan, Alaska)

Nautical Miles	about 635
Duration of trip	16 days
Engine hours	91
Average cruising hours per day	5.7
Average distance covered per day	40 miles
Total fuel consumption	191 gallons

Paul Terdal
Portland, Oregon, to Glacier Bay National Park
Vessel: Nautical Dreamer
(1978 Ericson 35-foot sailboat)

Paul Terdal, my 25-year-old son, and four companions crossed the Columbia River bar in a 35-foot sailboat, then traveled up the Washington coast. They encountered stiff northwest winds and waves of six to eight feet during most of their cruise on the outside of the Washington coast. However, the sea conditions were well within acceptable limits for their vessel. After making the turn at Cape Flattery, they headed into the Strait of Juan de Fuca and entered the harbor at Victoria, B.C. They began the Inside Passage portion of their journey at Victoria and continued on up and spent a full week at their northernmost destination—Glacier Bay National Park. Their account is of special interest because, on their return from Alaska, they chose the outside route and traveled over 700 miles at sea, which brought them past the Queen Charlotte Islands, the west side of Vancouver Island and on down the Washington coast before re-entering the Columbia River. Their account creates a perspective for those who want to make that level of a trip.

This summary reviews the log of their trip from Victoria to Ketchikan, Alaska. The outside portion of their trip is contained in the chapter, "The Outside Passage to Alaska."

Summary of trip by Paul Terdal and companions
(Victoria, B.C., to Ketchikan, Alaska)

Nautical Miles	about 635
Duration of trip	13 days
Engine hours	126
Average cruising hours per day	9.7 hours
Average distance covered per day	49 miles
Total fuel consumption	90 gallons

Leif and Marge Terdal
Port Townsend, Washington, to Glacier Bay National Park
Vessel: Second Effort
(26-foot Clipper Craft Cruiser)

The vessel I have used on four trips to Alaska is a modified dory design with a substantial cabin, considering the length of the boat. The boat is powered by a four-cylinder Volvo-Penta diesel engine with a duo-prop outdrive propulsion system. I steer the boat from inside the small pilot house, which is handy when the weather is cold, wet and windy. The boat is equipped with a Dickenson diesel heater, a head, and a small galley. Although not a live-aboard (I think of it as a camp-aboard), the boat is comfortable for two persons to take an extended trip. I can cruise at 16 knots and use about four gallons of diesel fuel per hour. I chose a trailerable boat so I could haul it to the Puget Sound and start the trip from the protected waters of the Inside Passage and avoid the more dangerous waters of the Oregon and Washington coasts.

My boating experiences are incorporated within two chapters, "The Canadian Inside Passage" and "The Alaskan Inside Passage." The following is a summary of log information of the portion of the trip from Port Townsend, Washington, to Ketchikan, Alaska.

Summary of trip by Leif Terdal
(Port Townsend, Washington, to Ketchikan, Alaska)

Nautical Miles   about 635
Duration of trip   6 days
Engine hours   45

Average cruising hours per day	7.5
Average distance covered per day	106 miles
Total fuel consumption	185 gallons

Princess Cruises, Los Angeles
Vancouver, British Columbia, to Ketchikan, Alaska
Vessel: Sky Princess

The Sky Princess is a cruise ship that regularly takes passengers from Vancouver, B.C., to Alaska. The ship's gross tonnage is 43,692 tons, and its length is 788 feet 9 inches. The main engine has 32,200 horsepower. The cruise ship carries 1350 passengers and a crew of 540. Traveling north from Vancouver, B.C., the first stop for this ship is Ketchikan, Alaska. The total distance for this section of the cruise is 565.5 nautical miles. This is a bit shorter than for private boaters who travel from ports farther south than Vancouver. In most respects, the route and the distance traveled by cruise ships is very similar to that taken by private boaters who cruise the Inside Passage. A major difference is that cruise ships do not let passengers disembark in small towns or pause to anchor in isolated coves or inlets.

From Ketchikan, Sky Princess proceeded on to Juneau and, after a stopover of 16 hours, continued on to Skagway. After a stopover of 12 hours, Sky Princess traveled from Skagway to Yakutat Bay. The vessel spent two hours so the passengers could view the Hubbard Glacier. Sky Princess continued on and entered College Fjord, where she slowed down so the passengers could view Harvard Glacier. From Harvard Glacier the cruise ship traveled on to Seward. The Sky Princess traveled a total of 1,732 miles from Vancouver, B.C., to Seward, Alaska.

Summary of the Cruise of the Sky Princess
(Port Angeles, Washington, to Ketchikan, Alaska)

Nautical Miles   565.5
Duration of trip   36 hours (nonstop)
Engine hours   36
Cruising speed   16 knots
Total fuel consumption   70,452 gallons

The Right Stuff

The five private boats described in the previous chapter provide a good way to consider the pros and cons of different types of boats and engine configurations for a cruise to Alaska. While there is truth to the adage that there is no perfect boat, the best way to determine suitability is to consider whether or not your choice in a boat is a good match for your long-distance cruising needs. Each of the five boats described above is considered against the standard of the personal goals of the owner-operators. Let's consider vessel speed, hull type, engine options, fuel capacity and cruising range, and vessel amenities. Finally, let's review the all-important phase of passage planning your cruise to Alaska.

Vessel speed

Vessel speed by itself may not be important, but it does make a difference. Cruising by sailboat is a popular way to cruise to Alaska, but the great majority of sailboaters who travel north along the Inside Passage motor rather than sail about 95 percent of the time and at an average of about five to seven knots. Boaters with displacement trawlers also go slowly and generally average about seven to 11 knots. As a rule of thumb, five knots is a good minimum speed to be able to maintain while cruising to Alaska, and the vessel should have at least that capacity.

If a speed of five knots is sufficient (and it is), when does extra speed make a real difference? Aside from the obvious difference in travel time to cover a long-distance cruise, there are three conditions under which increased speed can play an important part: 1. Tidal current, 2. Windows of opportunity between weather systems, and 3. Fatigue.

1. Tidal current

Tidal currents going either with or against a boater are a factor the entire length of the Canadian and Alaskan Inside Passage. Boaters whose vessels cruise at five knots need to plan their cruising time with tide and current in mind. The account of Leif Knutsen, described above, provides day-to-day details of starting time and length of cruise. Of course, the times given apply only to the tides and currents that were in force during his trip, but they illustrate a point. He made every effort to go with the current, and that often made for predawn departures. Because winds going in one direction and current going in the opposite direction will accentuate wave action, early departures often provide cruising time before "fair-weather winds" from the north develop. This again puts pressure on the boater for early departures.

While all boaters need to plan departure times in areas of strong to extremely strong currents, such as at Dodd Narrows, Seymour Narrows, Foggy Bay and Wrangell Narrows, boaters with comparatively slow boats need to make accommodations to the effects of currents for the entire voyage.

2. Windows of opportunity

A major advantage of a boat with speed occurs when there is a window of good weather and sea conditions against a forecast of a significant downturn in the weather. This has happened to me several times, but let me share one example. Once my wife and I were on our way south to return to the Puget Sound area and were about to leave Ketchikan for Prince Rupert. We had just fueled up at the main fuel dock at the south end of Ketchikan. The marine weather then issued a weather advisory for the Dixon Entrance, forecasting winds increasing to 30-plus knots from the southeast. That meant we could be exposed to strong winds and waves against us for a significant open-ocean crossing. Since the U.S. Coast Guard station was in close proximity to the fuel dock, I ran over for a more detailed weather briefing. A Coast Guardsman took me to a weather room with a wall of maps and reviewed the current status and forecast. He asked me about the speed of my boat. When I explained that our boat could cruise at 16 knots, he said that the conditions were still calm and that it was possible to run the entire distance before the winds developed. Within 15 minutes we were on our way, and we arrived safely in Prince Rupert within six hours. The winds picked up a couple of hours after we arrived in Prince Rupert.

3. Fatigue

A third reason to opt for a boat with speed is to limit cruising time. For example, Andy and Loris Peace from Idaho wanted to keep cruising time at a minimum and for them a fast boat made that possible. On most days they limited travel time to a few hours a day and enjoyed the stops. Even when they undertook lengthy crossings, such as the passage over Queen Charlotte Sound and the passage across the Dixon Entrance, they covered the distance in about six hours, whereas displacement-type sailboats and trawlers would have required two to three times as long. On a related point, I have spoken to many boaters who have told me they missed opportunities to visit key places, such as Tracy Arm, because they felt their very slow boats would take too much time.

Hull Type and Long-Range Cruising

All five boats (three power boats and two sailboats) described in Chapter One are suitable for cruising the Inside Passage. However, none of the three power boats are suitable for long-range cruising in the ocean of the Pacific Northwest or North Pacific—the Outside Passage. Each would be able to handle what are referred to as day trips into the Pacific, i.e., leaving one port and returning to the same port later in the day, assuming favorable weather conditions. However, none of them would be suitable for traveling up the coast, leaving one port and entering another up the line. Sailboats, especially blue-water sailboats designed for long-range ocean cruising, while comparatively slow are superior to power boats in rough seas, either going into the waves or handling following seas.

Any vessel going up the Inside Passage should be able to handle an hour or so of choppy sea conditions with steep waves of three or four feet. Such choppy seas can develop after a favorable start. While seas with steep waves of four feet are not a problem for a well-built sailboat, a trailerable power boat would also need to be able to handle such a situation in order to be suitable for cruising the Inside Passage.

Relatively small, low-horsepower-displacement or semidisplacement cruising boats would be very suitable for long-distance cruising in sheltered passages. Vessels of this type are very common in Europe and would be excellent for cruising to Alaska. Considering their length, displacement-hull boats handle rough waters better than lighter, planing-hull vessels. However, relatively small, displacement boats (less than 30 feet) are not popular in the United States. The 26-foot Nordic Tug powered by a Yanmar diesel is a great example. However, that model is no longer available. The smallest Nordic Tug currently available is 32 feet and cannot be considered a trailerable boat. If you live in California or Texas or any place remote from Puget Sound and have such a boat, you have the problem of getting your very suitable trawler to a starting point to begin the Inside Passage. The displacement boat designed by Leif Knutsen points out the possibilities of small, low-horsepower boats for economical long-range cruising in protected waters.

Engine Considerations

A power boat less than 30 feet long can easily be powered by a high-horsepower outboard or by an inboard-outdrive powered by either a gas or diesel engine. Without question, large, heavy boats are much better suited for diesel power than gas. The argument can be made for using diesel versus gas in a trailerable boat. I chose a diesel engine for my 26-foot cruiser because I plan to use the boat extensively. I have put on over 8000 miles of boating within the Inside Passage in a four-year time frame and plan to put on many more miles. Lower fuel costs and longer engine life should more than make up for the initial higher engine cost. The cost difference would not be recouped if a boater used his vessel less than 100 hours a year.

Even in cases of many hours of engine use per year, other considerations may cause one to opt for another engine type. For example, I spoke with the owner of a 26-foot outboard-powered charter boat in Wrangell, Alaska, which used a 250-horsepower Yamaha with a ten-horsepower, four-stroke Yamaha for trolling. He told me he averages 60 to 100 miles per day from mid-May through the end of August. With that amount of fuel use and engine hours, I asked him why he didn't install a diesel engine. He replied, "I can afford an engine breakdown, but I can not afford being tied at a dock while waiting for repairs."

He explained that most of his customers fly up from the lower 48 states and book him for three or more days at a time. The whole trip is expensive for them, and he said he couldn't let them down with an engine failure that took days, even weeks to repair. He told me he buys two big outboards every four years and has one on reserve as a backup. If his primary engine fails, he replaces it and continues on without missing a day of fishing. After four years he replaces both engines (sooner if necessary).

There are an impressive and wide array of new offerings in marine engines, both gas and diesel inboards as well as outboards. The new, large-horsepower, four-stroke outboard motors should be an excellent match for planing boats up to about 28 feet. In addition, the low-horsepower, high-thrust, four-stroke outboards, such as the ten-horsepower Yamaha is excellent as a trolling engine or backup motor on a cruiser up to 30 feet.

The main point about boat and engine match is not to underpower a boat with a planing hull. The boat should have sufficient power to get it on plane without undue stress on the engine. Similarly, there is no point in overpowering a boat with a displacement-type hull. However, the engine should be sufficient to bring the boat to a cruising hull speed at a good deal less than wide-open throttle.

Fuel Capacity and Cruising Range

To cruise the Inside Passage, a vessel should have a cruising range of at least 200 miles, with a reserve of about 15 percent. It is important to evaluate fuel consumption and range under the load conditions that will apply to your vessel on your extended cruise trip.

I am repeatedly reminded that one of the drawbacks to a small boat on a big cruise is that the same basic equipment is required as on much larger boats. Let's list a few.

All boats, regardless of size, must have on board required Coast Guard equipment such as life jackets, flares, fire extinguishers, etc. Boating equipment needed for extended cruising includes the following: two sets of anchors, chain and rope, a dinghy, tools, navigational charts, spare parts such as extra propellers, fuel and oil filters. Living on a boat means having on board groceries, dishes and utensils, clothing, sleeping gear, cleaning supplies, a bucket and water hose. Other necessities include fishing gear, books, games and a first aid kit. All this takes space—which is at a premium on small boats—and adds weight. The extra weight takes a toll on boat speed, fuel economy and range. Some boaters add jerry cans with extra fuel, and that adds even more weight.

The worst combination I have seen for boat size, engine configuration and vessel overload was in Ketchikan. I walked over to a boat which was docked near mine and I looked in amazement. The boat was sitting so low in the water I thought the owner might be hiding an elephant on board. Just then the owner stepped out of his cabin and we chatted. His boat was a 28-foot cabin cruiser powered with twin gas inboard-outdrives. Attached to the stern was a large dinghy with a ten-horsepower outboard. He had two bicycles tied on the bow and 12 jerry cans positioned at different places to carry extra fuel. He had come with his family of four from the Puget Sound area and said his fuel consumption averaged ten gallons of gas per hour at a speed of eight knots (about 790 gallons of fuel one way from Puget Sound to Ketchikan). With the weight overload he could not bring his boat up to a plane, and frankly, an overloaded boat is a hazard in rough-water conditions. To make things worse, one of his engines began to overheat while en route from Prince Rupert to Ketchikan and ran rough. The last time I saw him he told me that the engine repair would take about three weeks and he had decided to instead make arrangements to have his boat barged back to the Seattle area. His dilemma illustrates how important it is with a trailerable boat to keep extra weight to a minimum and to take into account the weight of the vessel when determining boat speed, handling characteristics, and range.

Vessel Amenities

For a trailerable cruiser to be suitable for a two-month or more long-distance cruise for two people, it should have the following amenities:

1. The cabin should be absolutely watertight, and the cockpit should be self-bailing, i.e., rainwater should drain off the deck and overboard, and not into the bilge.
2. Sleeping quarters should be comfortable with good-quality cushions.
3. The boat should have toilet facilities in a small enclosure with privacy, rather than a "port-a-potty" tucked under the V-bunk.

4. The cabin should have a heater that is reliable and safe.
5. The galley should be sufficient to prepare hot and cold, full-course meals. Refrigeration is necessary, but it can consist of an ice cooler rather than an AC/DC refrigerator.
6. Personal hygiene and bathing can be handled by heating water and taking sponge baths; a shower with hot and cold running water, though nice, is not necessary.
7. The cabin should have a comfortable place to accommodate a variety of activities like reading, talking, reviewing charts, etc.

Essential equipment for an extended cruise to Alaska, in addition to safety equipment required by the U.S. Coast Guard:

Two sets of anchor and chain,
    each with about 300 feet of rope
A dinghy
VHF radio
Navigational charts
Compass
Depth finder
Global Positioning System (GPS)
Radar reflector (radar is highly recommended)

Passage Planning Your Cruise to Alaska

Undertaking an extended cruise up the Canadian Inside Passage to Alaska and back, along with allowing time to cruise the Alaskan waters, requires a time commitment of about two months or more. It is essential to plan well for such a trip and there are a number of considerations to think through. Let's consider time constraints.

If you wish to visit Glacier Bay National Park during the summer months (June through August), you will need a permit in advance. Apply for a permit that fits your plans, and then work around it. Aside from Glacier Bay, think about the other places you want to explore in S.E. Alaska and in the Canadian waters. Within S.E. Alaska, for example, you may want to explore such vastly beautiful and pristine places as the following: Misty Fjord National Monument; the fjords, glaciers and waterfalls in Tracy Arm and Endicott Arm; the bear observatories, such as those at Pack Creek (permit required) and Anan Creek; some of the small cities in Alaska such as Wrangell, Petersburg, Haines, Skagway, and Sitka, as well as the two major tourist attractions of Ketchikan and Juneau. To a great extent, the geography of S.E. Alaska and the waters of the Inside Passage will help you to organize your plans. Reviewing the maps and charts, thinking through a time frame for your trip, and figuring out in advance end points for each cruising day, including at which harbor or anchorage to spend each night, will make your trip easier and more enjoyable.

Perhaps the most basic time consideration is how far you plan to cruise each day (given reasonable weather and sea conditions). This depends directly on the speed of your boat and your tolerance for handling a boat without becoming too fatigued. These two considerations are why I detailed the accounts of five boaters who cruised the Inside Passage to Alaska. Some boaters are perfectly comfortable cruising 12 hours a day for days on end. Others do much better with more limited goals for cruising time and miles covered per day. The best rule of thumb is to plan an extended cruise within your comfort level and that of your crew or companions, as well as keeping within the cruising speed and seaworthiness of your boat.

Making the Plan

Arm yourself with a note pad and pen and reference materials. The reference materials include navigational charts that fully cover the cruise you plan to take. Tide and current tables are necessary. The most compelling reason to review tide and current tables is that portions of a passage include waters that are impassable at certain times, offering narrow windows of time to make a safe passage. Seymour Narrows in B.C. is one example. In such a case it is important to consider a good time for a safe passage and then work backward to your departure time so that you arrive at an optimal time. Even when such a restriction does not exist, paying attention to tide and currents helps you plan your departures each day to take advantage of the tidal flow going in your direction, especially important for vessels with a slow cruising speed of about five knots. Faster boats need not bother with tidal currents of one to three knots, but not even the big cruise ships ignore the occasions when tidal currents exceed 12 knots.

Other Reference Materials

There are several books that provide useful information on how to plan for a cruise up the Inside Passage. I recommend that you purchase each of the following:

Charlie's Charts North to Alaska (Victoria, B.C., to Glacier Bay, Alaska), by C.E. Wood. This excellent guide was first published in 1986 and revised in 1995. Not meant to be a substitute for navigational charts, it provides excellent information about harbors and anchorages along the entire route, as well as information about potential hazards, such as rocks near certain entrances, which channels should only be entered during high slack, etc.

The *Waggoner Cruising Guide* is the best-selling Northwest cruising guide and provides skippers with cruising information on the waters from South Puget Sound to Prince Rupert. It provides a comprehensive description of waterways, bays and marinas as well as pointers on how best to handle certain potentially difficult passages. The book is not intended to be a substitute for official government charts, tide and current tables. You can obtain a copy by writing:

Waggoner Cruising Guide
Robert Hale & Co. Inc.
1803 132nd Ave. N.E, Suite 4
Bellevue, WA 98005-2261

The Marine Atlas Volume I (Olympia to Malcolm Island) and *The Marine Atlas Volume II* (Port Hardy to Skagway) provide maps of the entire route from Puget Sound to Skagway and other places in Alaska, such as Glacier Bay and Sitka. It is useful in that it proves a quick overview of distances between destination points throughout the Inside Passage, as well as recommended magnetic course readings to follow during the passage. Again, it is not a substitute for government navigational charts. The two volumes are very useful, in addition to the references mentioned above, in planning day-to-day segments of an extended cruise.

Make A Written Plan for Phase I of Your Cruise to Alaska

After considering the amount of time available to you and your personal objectives of your trip, construct a written plan. Think of Ketchikan, Alaska, as your destination for Phase I. For each cruising day, decide on a departure time, an average cruising speed, and a destination point, such as a marina or a suitable anchorage. Of course, weather can change plans. However, in my five cruises to Alaska, I have found that in nine days out of ten, I am able to reach a planned destination point without undue difficulty. On the other days I cut short the day's travel and pull into what I consider a "plan B" marina or anchorage, because weather conditions developed that dictated cutting that day's trip short. In discussions with dozens of boaters who have cruised the Inside Passage to Alaska, I've heard the same thing—they are usually able to reach a planned day's destination without great difficulty. It is important to allow a certain number of days to remain in dock or anchorage because of inclement weather. This is especially true if you have a specific date to enter a place such as Glacier Bay. On that point, a staff person at Glacier Bay told me that they get a number of calls from permit holders each year who advise they will arrive in Glacier Bay earlier than expected. They get fewer calls from boaters saying that weather conditions will delay their entry to the park. All this supports the wisdom of making a plan and following it.

Passage Notes

It is useful to record in your written plan what are referred to as "passage notes." These notes would include any points of interest that you will pass on a particular day's cruise, as well as any hazards, such as shoals, reefs, or rocks that may be below the surface at certain times during tide changes. Young children as well as adult companions will enjoy anticipating these potential hazards as well as a safe passage around them. Along the same line, children usually enjoy anticipating and then spotting navigational aids, such as buoys and lighthouses.

I strongly recommend that you allow time during a day's travel to stop short of your destination point, get off the boat, and visit some major points of interest. In my chapters on both the Canadian and Alaskan portions of the Inside Passage, I highlight places of interest that may or may not be an end point for a given day but are well worth a visit.

Once you arrive in Ketchikan, which is truly a major accomplishment, review the places and activities you want to experience and work out a plan for the rest of your trip.

The Outside Passage: Travel by Land or Sea?

If you live outside the waters of Puget Sound and plan to cruise to Alaska, consider the option of travel by land as well as travel by sea to get your boat to a starting point to begin the Inside Passage journey. Consider each of the following three options:

By Land: Trailer your boat or hire a professional trucker to haul it to a port within Puget Sound.

For hauling your own boat, assuming it is trailerable, do you own a tow vehicle capable of hauling such a load? It may make sense to own a tow rig if you plan to cruise waters that are far apart from each other—for example, the Inside Passage to Alaska one year and Baja or Lake Powell the next. In my case I own a trailerable boat and a suitable heavy-duty, double-axle trailer with surge brakes. I decided against purchasing a heavy-duty tow vehicle because my present requirements call for towing the boat only a few hundred miles per year. In the future I may purchase a substantial tow vehicle if I plan to explore waters far removed from the Northwest. It costs me about a thousand dollars each season to hire someone to haul my boat from Oregon to Port Townsend, Washington, and to haul it out at the end of the season and return it. Your situation may be different and would depend on the size (length and width) of your boat and travel distance from your residence to a port within Puget Sound.

It is interesting to consider the size of your boat depending upon whether it is in the ocean or on the highway. My 26-foot boat is a small boat when I am cruising to Alaska. It can be called a minicruiser or pocket cruiser. On the highway it is a maxitrailerable boat. At the modest weight of 4,500 pounds, it is too heavy to be hauled by a family vehicle and would require a heavy-duty pickup truck or a large SUV.

Once the weight of a boat reaches 10,000 pounds (still modest as boats go), the best option is probably to hire a professional trucker. When I meet boaters along the Inside Passage to Alaska with boat numbers far removed from the West Coast, I always ask them how they got their boats to the Puget Sound. A couple from Georgia with a 42-foot sailboat said they had the boat trucked across the country to Seattle. I have heard the same from boaters I encountered from Texas, Rhode Island, West Virginia and Georgia. If you are considering having your boat hauled by a professional trucker, check with your own network of boaters and cruisers. Most marinas have personnel with expertise and experience in working with professional boat haulers.

By Sea: Hire an experienced captain to be in charge of running your boat up north—on the outside—and to bring your vessel to a port where you can begin cruising the Inside Passage.

As I described above in the chapter "Six Boats, One Passage," Peter and Natalie Bates had a successful trip cruising their 35-foot motor sailor from Port Angeles, Washington, to Glacier Bay. With them were their two young daughters and Natalie's father, Bob. After purchasing their motor sailor in Portland, Oregon, they decided to run their boat up the outside of the Washington coast, rather than have their large and heavy vessel trucked commercially to Anacortes, Washington. Their decision was based on cost as well as the time involved in removing the mast for the truck haul and having to reassemble the mast and all the rigging when the vessel was relaunched. The decision to hire a captain for the section along the Washington coast was a wise one considering that neither Peter nor Natalie had experience boating in the Pacific. Peter Bates contacted an experienced captain he had met in Portland who agreed to help them travel up the outside of the Washington coast. Their account of the journey provides a helpful look at the ocean conditions that can be expected along the Oregon and Washington coast and gives insight on why it is worth considering alternatives to a do-it-yourself trip along the outside. The young children were not on board during this part of the trip.

Fair-Weather Sailing: The Washington Coast

In the words of Peter Bates: We fueled up in Astoria, Oregon, and headed across the Columbia River bar at 8 a.m. on July 1. The bar itself was a breeze. The seas were calm and pleasant and the skies sunny and clear. We followed the buoy line, staying just south of the line of black buoys and cleared all of them before turning north. Very soon the winds from the northwest picked up and the seas got bigger with the waves steep and close together. It was uncomfortable and I was terrified, out of my wits. Gary, the captain, was cool about it. He was comfortable and didn't think the seas were unusual for the Oregon-Washington coast. The wind increased after noon and was blowing at about 30 knots. These are called fair-weather winds coming from the north and northwest. From time to time a big wave would hit us and roll the boat so hard over, I was certain we would take on too much water and sink.

When nightfall came, the winds subsided and the seas settled, but the visibility was very poor. There was no moon, no lights on the horizon, and no other boats in the area. We were steering strictly by compass. Our captain divided the night shift into three watches, with my father-in-law taking the second watch. About half an hour into his watch, he called out to say that our boat was going around in circles. He said the steering system had broken down. This brought all of us on top to the pilot house. Even Gary was really rattled, and my fear went way up. I checked the main compass at the binnacle; it was stable, which meant the little compass in the pilot house was erratic. In the blackness of the night, with no other visible cues, we were disoriented as to direction by a defective compass. What a relief! We had a reliable compass at the binnacle, and we could get readings over ground from our GPS. We were free to ignore the unstable readings of the compass in the pilot house; the accuracy of the compass had not made my very long list of high-priority things to check before our trip. At any rate, Gary, Bob and I stayed together at the helm and talked things over. Soon we were all confident we were proceeding on course.

The next morning the seas were calm and it was gorgeous. As we went around Cape Flattery and entered the Strait of Juan de Fuca, we were faced with a strong ebb current going against us. At the same time the northwest winds picked up again as we were beating against the current. We met up with enormous rollers, made slow progress, and were uncomfortable. We were also worried about the tremendous freight traffic that was constant in the area; and those ships move very fast.

We finally made landfall in Port Angeles late that afternoon, 36 hours after we left Astoria. The Outside Passage up the Washington coast and around Cape Flattery was a real shakedown for us; but the engine was flawless—it never missed a beat. In spite of water and spray that came over our boat nearly continuously in the rough seas, essentially no water came into the boat cabin or into bilge. I learned the true meaning of a blue-water boat.

Author's Note: Some thoughts about cruising the Outside Passage up the Oregon-Washington coast:

As you read about the voyage of the Bateses along the Washington coast, you may have wondered why they stayed out at sea during the tough conditions. What options did they have?

There are few harbors off the Oregon-Washington coast. Once a boater leaves the mouth of the Columbia River and heads north, the next harbor is Grays Harbor—about 40 miles north. An important harbor for commercial fishing vessels, Grays Harbor presents difficulties coming in and out of it. If your intent is to travel on to Alaska, there is no point in stopping here. This is especially true if ocean conditions are bad with rough seas. Staying out at sea and progressing north is usually the best option.

After Grays Harbor, the next harbor (and the only other one along the Washington coast) is La Push, which is about 60 miles north of Grays Harbor and 35 miles south of Cape Flattery. This harbor is worth considering as a stopover during conditions of strong northwest winds. Of all the harbors along the Oregon-Washington coast, this small harbor is the safest to enter from the ocean during conditions of strong northwest winds. James Island, just offshore of the mouth of Quillayute River, provides a good buffer against swells from the northwest. However, the entrance is extremely dangerous when strong winds are from the south or southwest. The Bateses' vessel happened to be offshore of La Push at night and they had no reason to interrupt their passage to the north. All things considered, Peter, his father-in-law, and their captain did well to stay out at sea and hold the course.

In summary, there are relatively few harbors off the Oregon-Washington coast, and none of them are deep-water harbors. Because all the harbor entrances are shallow, ocean swells build up as they approach shore and often create dangerous bar conditions. This is especially true during ebb tides, when currents move from the harbors out to the seas and meet the waves moving towards shore. The weather in the Pacific Northwest has a very dominant summer weather pattern consisting of cool, strong breezes from the northwest. These winds generally start in the morning and build up during the day and settle somewhat at night, then start again the next day. Although they typically blow at 25 to 35 knots, these winds can exceed 40 knots. Heading into these seas for a passage that lasts more than a day and a night is tiring and uncomfortable. If one leaves a Pacific port much farther to the south—for example, from San Francisco—the Outside Passage could easily last seven to ten days before the boater enters the Strait of Juan de Fuca and can begin the calmer journey of the Inside Passage.

If you and your crew are experienced to handle the outside waters off Oregon and Washington, go for it.

Perhaps the only reason for considering taking the Outside Passage to Alaska is that you are already familiar with long-distance blue-water cruising. Three things need to be in place to accomplish an extended Outside Passage cruise to Alaska: 1) a vessel with a sound and seaworthy hull; 2) a reliable propulsion system (sail or power); and, 3) an experienced crew familiar with the sea conditions likely to be encountered. The same three points would need to be in place if you were to sail from a West Coast port to Hawaii. It is vital that you understand the seaworthiness of your boat, your experience and that of your crew, and the hazards of the journey. To overrate your ability or underrate the risk could be deadly.

The following account is of a trip taken by Paul Terdal and some companions to Glacier Bay, Alaska, from Astoria, Oregon. The Alaskan trip was a two-month segment of a voyage that ended in Providence, Rhode Island, after 11 months and about 11,000 miles.

Proposed Route and Time Frame

In the words of Paul Terdal: My plan was to travel from Astoria, Oregon, to Alaska and then on down the West Coast, through the Panama Canal, cruising the Caribbean Sea and then up the Atlantic coast. A major consideration for such a lengthy trip covering a wide range of areas is to determine a schedule that places the vessel in a region during that region's good-weather period. For example, it is important not to cruise in the Pacific Northwest during the fall and winter storm season. Likewise, it is important not to enter Mexican waters until after the hurricane season ends around the first of November. My travel plans were also set to accommodate a trip to Glacier Bay. Only 25 private boats are allowed at any time in this national park, and I was able to obtain a permit. I planned to arrive at Glacier Bay 30 days after leaving Astoria, Oregon. That time frame permitted me allowances for weather problems, crew performance matters, vessel maintenance and, most important, time to experience the Canadian and Alaskan waters, scenery and wildlife.

The boat:

My boat, the Nautical Dreamer, a 35-foot sailboat (a 1978 Ericson 35), is a well-equipped, seaworthy boat that was designed for ocean sailing. The previous owner sailed her as far as Central America and used her regularly for ocean races up the coast of Washington State. When I purchased the boat, it was very well equipped and laid out for ocean sailing. I did replace the Westerbeke diesel with a new Yanmar diesel. I found that the boat handled very well, both under sail and under power.

The skipper:

I grew up on salmon fishing boats in waters off the Oregon coast. Starting at age 12, I worked summers as a deck hand on my father's commercial salmon troller, the Siglaos. I began sailing in 1987 and now devote the bulk of my free time to sailing, sailboat maintenance, and nautical self-education.

Expectation of crew members:

I was fortunate to find a group of people to sail with me to Alaska and back, and who contributed to the expenses of operating and maintaining the boat. I sought crew members who were able to be partners, active members of a team rather than subservient crew. By and large we made decisions by consensus; however, as captain, I had both a legal and moral responsibility to have the last word when necessary.

Passage north from Astoria up the Washington Coast:

My plan was to cross the Columbia River bar, sail up the Washington coast, enter the Strait of Juan de Fuca and sail to Victoria, B.C. That trip would be about 250 miles and take about 50 hours; I hoped to complete that portion of the journey nonstop. We left Astoria on June 17, 1993, and crossed the Columbia river bar without difficulty. We did encounter northwest winds of about 25 knots during the afternoon and motored into seas of about six feet. The waves were steep, but the boat handled well. One crew member became very seasick. The only feasible port for me to enter was the harbor at La Push, Washington. Roger, our seasick crew member, toughed it out for just over 28 hours. We stayed overnight at La Push and Roger's wife drove up from Portland to pick him up. We left the next day and continued on. We passed Cape Flattery on the northwest tip of the Washington coast and sailed into the Strait of Juan de Fuca. We encountered some large swells within the Strait but had no difficulty. We arrived at Victoria after traveling about 52 hours of boating time from Astoria. A good rule of thumb for sailing is to figure about 120 miles of travel for each 24 hours. From Victoria we traveled the Inside Passage and encountered no rough seas that were anything like the Washington coast or the west portion of the Strait of Juan de Fuca. In this chapter I will limit my comments to boating along the Outside Passage and forego descriptions of the wonderful days we spent exploring the cruising waters in Canada and in Southeast Alaska.

The Outside Passage from Prince Rupert, B.C., to San Diego, California

The sailing distance from Prince Rupert, B.C., to San Diego is about 1900 miles. To aid me in my planning, I consider the trip to consist of five legs: 1) Prince Rupert, B.C., to the Queen Charlotte Islands; 2) the Queen Charlottes to the west coast of Vancouver Island; 3) Vancouver Island to Astoria, Oregon; 4) Astoria, Oregon, to Brookings, Oregon; and, 5) Brookings, Oregon, to San Diego.

Leg 1:
Prince Rupert, B.C., to the Queen Charlotte Islands

From Prince Rupert we took a route known as Venn Passage to get us past Digby Island into Chatham Sound; from there we proceeded west past Stephens Island and entered Hecate Strait. The sea conditions were rough. The wind was blowing steady at about 25 knots and the waves were six to eight feet and came at our beam. Since the winds were coming from the northwest and our direction was to our west, there was little we could do to position the boat for a smoother ride. The boat, however, handled nasty weather pretty well. The seas were also difficult because the ocean is fairly shallow between the Queen Charlottes and the mainland, and currents increase the wave action. Our initial destination was the fishing town of Skidgate on Graham Island. Coming into the harbor, it was important that we approached close to shore north of Skidgate and then proceeded south near shore. There is a reef offshore that is shallow and has claimed some boats. We spent one night at Skidgate and then proceeded south with the intention of covering the entire distance to Winter Harbor on the northwest side of Vancouver Island. We encountered winds that approached 40 knots and the seas were very difficult. We pulled into Luxana Bay on the south coast of the Queen Charlotte Islands. This offered complete protection. We waited out some bad weather for three days and tried to explore the island (Knight Island). The terrain was so overgrown with shrubs and trees, however, that we could not walk more than three miles in eight hours. Needless to say we struggled back and spent the rest of the waiting period on the boat.

Leg 2:
Queen Charlotte Islands
(Luxana Bay to Vancouver Island)

This leg of our trip was about 145 miles and took us to Winter Harbor. To our amazement and disappointment, the winds that blew so fierce several days earlier suddenly stopped. We motored the entire distance from Luxana Bay to Winter Harbor. The trip was smooth and comfortable, but to a sailer the trip was too quiet. The town of Winter Harbor is a commercial fishing town and is well supplied with fuel and other boating necessities. After a day we left Winter Harbor and sailed down the west side of Vancouver Island to Barkley Sound. This portion of the trip was about 183 miles and we had some good winds. Barkley Sound is a spectacular place and is a destination area for many boaters. Within the sound is Pacific Rim National Park, with about a thousand islands. We moored at Bamfield, which is at the southern part of the sound.

Leg 3:
Barkley Sound to Astoria, Oregon

This section of our trip took us across the west side of the Strait of Juan de Fuca and down the coast of Washington. We did not plan to enter a port on the Washington coast, as our planned destination was Astoria. The distance was about 200 miles and we covered the trip in about 30 hours, travelling with northwest winds and seas of six to eight feet.

Leg 4:
Astoria, Oregon, to Brookings, Oregon

This section of the Oregon coast is about 300 miles. Northwest winds are very common during the summer months. Some eight hours after leaving the Columbia River entrance, we approached a section just west of Tillamook Bay. The wind was blowing steadily at about 25 to 30 knots and we were making excellent progress. It is much easier, of course, to sail with the wind then against it. However, there are hazards when sailing with the wind. I tried to maximize speed by going as close as possible straight downwind, rather than tacking back and forth. Unfortunately, I caught a wave that positioned the boat in such a way that the mainsail moved in an instant from port to starboard. The sail moved across with such force that the boom snapped. It made a tremendous bang. With the mainsail out of commision I had to resort to the diesel engine. I pulled into Coos Bay, on the southern Oregon coast, and radioed an order for a new boom to be delivered to San Diego. I picked it up when I arrived there about two weeks later.

Leg 5:
Coos Bay, Oregon, to San Diego

This distance is about 850 miles and we covered the journey in about 120 sailing hours. I decided against extended overnight cruising and limited daily travel time to about six to 15 hours. On the way down we stopped and moored (or anchored) at the following places: Eureka, Shelter Cove, Fort Bragg, Bodega Bay, Half Moon Bay, Monterey, San Simeon, Port San Luis, Lojo Anchorage, Channel Islands Marina, Long Beach, and Mission Bay (San Diego). As we travelled south I was impressed with the change in the offshore ocean conditions about halfway down California. The waters off Washington, Oregon and northern California are not good cruising waters. The winds are too strong and there is no protection from strong ocean swells. Once a boater reaches Point Conception conditions improve. The winds are not as consistently strong, and the water temperature is warmer. Southern California truly has much to offer boaters who like ocean cruising; in contrast, the offshore waters of the Northwest are tougher.

Northwest to Alaska: British Columbia and the Canadian Inside Passage

One of the secrets to a successful cruise to Alaska in a small boat (e.g., trailerable) is appreciating the ability to take advantage of opportunities to get off your boat. A 26- to 30-foot boat (sailboat or small cruiser) is not a liveaboard, although it can accommodate, with various degrees of discomfort, on-board camping for weeks or months. After a day of cruising, you don't ask your wife, "Dear, which of the seven dining areas on board would you prefer this evening?" Other options, which are available on cruise ships, are also nonexistent, such as movies, a dance floor, or hot tubs. By cruising in your small boat, you give up the entertainment options available on board cruise ships. What you gain, however, is the opportunity to personalize your adventure experience, including the chance to get off your boat and experience the landscape that is such a part of the beauty of the Inside Passage in both Canada and Alaska.

Depending on how far north you travel, you and your partner can expect to:

1. See wilderness settings, including snow-capped mountains, deep fjords, waterfalls, icebergs and glaciers

2. Observe bountiful wildlife, including many varieties of birds, marine mammals, such as whales, seals, sea lions, otters, and land mammals, especially bears
3. Visit small communities in B.C. and S.E. Alaska
4. Experience special wilderness areas, such as Misty Fjords National Monument, Tracy Arm, bear observatories, and the jewel of Southeast Alaska—Glacier Bay National Park
5. Catch fish
6. Learn to better appreciate Native culture in B.C. and S.E. Alaska
7. Begin to better understand the conflict between those who wish to expand the resource-dependent economy—timber industry, commercial fishing interests, and mining—in both B.C. and S.E. Alaska, and those who press for preservation of pristine wilderness and wildlife

This chapter on the Canadian Inside Passage and the next (on the Alaskan Inside Passage) are written to go beyond a description of "how to get there" and touch on what to see and experience along the way. This focus is especially developed for the more remote areas of the Canadian Inside Passage (between Port Hardy and Prince Rupert), as well as the wilderness areas in southeast Alaska apart from the key tourist cities.

The Canadian portion of the Inside Passage starts at the southern end of the Strait of Georgia, then follows a fairly narrow passageway from the northern end of the Strait of Georgia to the end of Vancouver Island. This can readily be understood as two legs of the journey, the first corresponding to the large, fairly open body of water (the Strait of

Georgia) and the second from Campbell River to Port Hardy. The term "legs" is not meant to correspond to days of travel, which can be individualized in many different ways.

Leg I:
Port Townsend, Washington, to Campbell River
(approximate distance 160 miles)

This portion of the trip involves crossing a portion of Puget Sound, then crossing the eastern part of the Strait of Juan de Fuca and proceeding up the entire portion of the Strait of Georgia. I have made this trip in two different ways:

1. Via Victoria

    One option is to cross the Strait of Juan de Fuca and head the short 35-mile distance to Victoria. When I take this route, I check in with Canadian customs upon arrival and spend the rest of the day and the night in Victoria. Victoria Harbor, in front of the beautiful Empress Hotel, is one of the best moorage bargains for transient boaters in a major port city anywhere. It costs me less than $15 (U.S.) for an overnight stay (a larger boat would cost proportionately more). The harbor gives access to the beautiful gardens, museums, restaurants, and stately buildings with a British flair in this great city.

    From Victoria (the next day) I have followed Haro Strait and Boundary Passage (U.S.- Canada border) between the Canadian Gulf Islands and the San Juan Islands. Just west of Patos Island (the northernmost island in the Washington San Juans), I head up through the main body of water in the Strait of Georgia. In about 20 miles I am positioned west of the Fraser River. This is the largest river in British

69

Columbia and has by far the largest salmon runs in B.C. From this spot, one can also see the great port city of Vancouver. Looking east, viewing the delta formed by the Fraser River and the outlines of Vancouver, reminds some of historic similarities and differences between the settlements and economic developments that occurred in Alaska and British Columbia. Alaska was purchased from Russia in 1867; Canada coincidentally became a nation independent of England also in 1867. British Columbia became a province of Canada in 1871 under the condition that B.C. would be linked to the east by railroad. The Canada Pacific Railroad was completed in 1885. The most western portion of the rail follows the Fraser River and ends in Vancouver. The rail line became the necessary link to export the vast amount of wheat grown in Saskatchewan to the west coast and to ship timber and salmon east from resource-rich British Columbia. The rail line made Vancouver a great port city and opened up the province of British Columbia to economic development—and wealth. The railroad and the port city of Vancouver contributed to British Columbia's showing a much faster population growth than occurred in Alaska.

When the Strait of Georgia has wind chop with waves of three to four feet, I slow the boat down and plan (when possible) to reach French Creek on Vancouver Island, west of Lasqueti Island. It takes me about ten hours to travel from Victoria to French Creek. French Creek has a very suitable harbor, fuel and good restaurants. The next day I head for Campbell River about three to four hours away.

2. Via South Pender Harbor

An alternative route to reach Campbell River from Port Townsend is to skip Victoria and proceed instead to Canadian customs at South Pender Harbor, then follow the protected route of Trincomali Channel to Gabriola Passage (or one of three other passages including Active Pass, Porlier Pass or Dodd Narrows) to enter the Strait of Georgia. With this route I have made the passage from Port Townsend to Campbell River in 11 hours—which saves two overnight stays. In large part the choice is based upon one's interest in visiting Victoria. Furthermore, this alternative route is especially worth choosing if the Strait of Georgia is windy and rough, because it provides a longer period of protection from rough seas.

Leg II:
Campbell River to Port Hardy
(approximate distance 108 miles)

But first: The Mountains and Ice Fields

Campbell River is right at latitude 50. This places this community south of Mt. Waddington, which, with an elevation of 13,177 feet, is the second highest mountain in British Columbia. A range of very high mountains continues on from latitude 50 for another 120 miles north. These highest mountains are not visible from a boat because the much smaller coastal ranges on the mainland block the view from sea level. It is interesting to remember and appreciate the dramatic fashion in which these very high mountains have left their imprint on the land and the inlets. The mountains still have massive snowfields and glaciers. During the ice ages they carved the fjords and inlets that are so pronounced. The area from Campbell River (to the north) represents a major transition in the sea and landscape of the Canadian portion of the Inside Passage. Some of the fjords go back more than 50 miles, and the dramatic cascading waterfalls are reminders of the work of massive and deep glaciers.

Latitude 50 and North: Two Routes

At the end of the Strait of Georgia, two routes proceed to the Queen Charlotte Strait and to the end of Vancouver Island. One route (called the northern route) winds through a series of passages around islands and ends up within the upper section of Johnstone Strait. The northern route is preferred when strong northwest winds are blowing down Johnstone Strait. Many writers of guidebooks about cruising the Inside Passage to Alaska recommend avoiding Johnstone Strait as much as possible because of the dangers of strong currents, rips, and difficult swirls. Walt Woodward, author of *How to Cruise to Alaska*, is especially strong in recommending that a boater take the northern route to avoid much of Johnstone Strait. I have taken the alternative route, the one going through Seymour Narrows.

Discovery Passage

I have gone through the Discovery Passage and Johnstone Strait route on my trips north to Alaska and on the return trips. I have encountered swirls, rips, and choppy waters but not to the point of the conditions being hazardous. A point to remember is that a combination of a strong ebb tide moving against strong winds from the northwest will create hazardous waters. I have not encountered that condition, but I recognize the possibility. Should the waters of Johnstone Strait become hazardous, there are options to pull into channels or inlets on the mainland side of Johnstone Strait. I prefer the route going through Seymour Narrows, simply because I am intrigued by the history of Ripple Rock and its removal from Seymour Narrows.

Discovery Passage and Seymour Narrows

Campbell River is eight miles south of Seymour Narrows. The shortness of that distance makes Campbell River a very convenient starting point to proceed, because it is essential to cross Seymour Narrows at slack tide or very near it. Although I can cruise at 16 knots, I leave Campbell River about an hour ahead of when slack tide will occur at the Narrows. At slack tide, crossing Seymour Narrows is pleasant and safe. In contrast, the Narrows during the midst of a bull ebb tide or bull flood tide has dangerous rips, whirlpools and swirls. In 1995, my son Paul and I crossed at slack tide, but we wanted to see the action that always develops at Seymour Narrows when the tidal current is strong. I pulled the boat into a cove north of the narrow entrance. Paul then lowered our dinghy, rowed to shore and hiked to the edge of a bluff on Maud Island. From this overlook he was able to view the development of strong whirlpools and swirls, but by agreement he left before the "main show." Some day we may repeat that experience with a longer stay. To view an entire sequence of the tidal flow and the turbulence, one would need to be dropped off with a dinghy at a slack tide and have the boater return at the next tide change for a pick up. The boat operator could spend the six hours or so of waiting at Brown Bay, a protected resort and marina about three miles north of Seymour

Narrows, before returning to pick up those who hiked to a viewpoint on Maud Island.

Ripple Rock: An Infamous Navigational Hazard

Prior to 1958, Seymour Narrows was a vastly more dangerous navigational hazard than it is now and had claimed over one hundred boats. In the early 1950s, several unsuccessful efforts were made to destroy Ripple Rock by positioning a drilling barge over the rock and drilling into it to set off an explosion. On the last effort with that strategy, the cables that had secured the barge broke and all nine men aboard were drowned. Engineering plans were then made to drill a tunnel from Maud Island straight down and then through the rock bed to a position under Ripple Rock. This effort took two and a half years. Finally, in the spring of 1958, an engineer detonated an explosion that blew rock and water ten thousand feet in the air. The powerful explosion was brought on by 1,300 carefully placed tons of TNT. A very severe navigational hazard was neutralized—at slack tide! Prior to 1958, this area was dangerous even during slack tide and catastrophic during strong tidal flows.

The best option going north is to cross Seymour Narrows at slack high tide because, as the current begins to ebb, the stream will go in your direction as you proceed north up the remainder of Discover Passage and into Johnstone Strait. This is especially important if your boat has a cruising speed of less than eight knots. The same principle holds on a return trip from an upstream anchorage, such as Kelsey Bay. It would be good to leave there at low tide and travel with the incoming tidal flow and plan to be at Seymour Narrows at slack high tide.

Chatham Point and the Entrance
to Johnstone Strait to Port Hardy

Chatham Point is at the northern end of Discovery Passage (on Vancouver Island) and has several lighthouse keepers' houses; the light itself (an important navigational marker) is about 1000 feet offshore and placed on Beaver Rock. This area is only about 12 miles from Seymour Narrows and connects with Johnstone Strait; it is about 88 miles from Port Hardy. On the Vancouver Island side of the strait, the only refuge west of Chatham Point and east of Alert Bay is Kelsey Bay. In fact, I normally plan to pull into the small harbor at Kelsey Bay, even under good conditions, spending the remainder of the day and then overnighting there, proceeding the next day to either Alert Bay or Port Hardy. This breaks up the trip and permits a morning start, which is less often associated with strong fair-weather northwest winds.

Kelsey Bay

Kelsey Bay is at the mouth of the Salmon River, an operation center for a very large-scale lumber operation. The shallow delta of the river has six large sunken freighters that form a breakwater for part of the timber operation. I have enjoyed walking the road from the bay to the small town about two miles inland. The town, which supports the timber operation, has a good grocery store and a small park. It's a great place to stretch the legs.

Robson Bight and Orca Whales

About 20 miles west of Kelsey Bay, in Johnstone Strait, is an area called Robson Bight. It is a protected area for a pod of Orca, or killer, whales. It is quite common to see Orca whales in this area. The rules for boating in the presence of Orca whales are no different in this area than any other place. We are not to pursue them, chase them, or go out of our way to follow them. In the Robson Bight area we are also not to beach our boat or launch a dinghy and go on shore. We have seen Orca whales in this area, but we have also seen them at some point en route from the Juan de Fuca Strait up into Alaska. However, Orca whales seem to be more prevalent in the Robson Bight area of Vancouver Island than in other places.

A most memorable occasion for my wife and me in encountering a pod of Orca whales occurred on a July day in 1995. It was high noon on a sunny day, with no wind and calm waters. We decided on a hot lunch, so I slowed the boat down to idle and kept it in gear to maintain steering and vessel control. We were between Hanson Island and Telegraph Cove, approximately ten miles east of Alert Bay. There were about four sea kayaks in the area; as we watched them, suddenly three Orca whales came into view and swam toward our slowly moving boat. One swam below our boat and surfaced within 30 feet of a kayaker, who himself was only 60 feet from us. The kayaker paused and took in the experience of his life—as did we. The whale remained motionless for a while on the surface, then continued on its way. When it comes to whale watching, it doesn't get much better than that!

Alert Bay

Alert Bay is located on banana-shaped Cormorant Island, situated 41 miles west of Kelsey Bay and 26 miles east of Port Hardy. At the center of the bay is a good breakwater and, behind it, docks and floats for fishing vessels and small craft. The town is the location for the Nimpish Indian Village. I enjoy stopping at Alert Bay to see the totem poles located on a Nimpish burial ground south of the town—about one-half mile from the docks. The burial grounds are sacred and understandably off limits, but the totem poles can be viewed quite well from the main road. There is also a cultural center about one-half mile northwest of the docks

U'Mista Cultural Centre Alert Bay, B.C.

The U'Mista Cultural Centre was incorporated in 1974 and established to carry out the following aims:

1. To collect, preserve and exhibit Native artifacts of cultural, artistic and historic value to the Kwagu't People
2. To promote and foster carving, dancing, ceremonials and other cultural and artistic activities engaged in by the Kwagu't people
3. To collect, record and make available information and records relating to the language and history of the Kwagu't people for the use of the Kwagu't people
4. To promote, build and maintain facilities for carrying out the above aims and objects
5. To recover from other institutions and individuals artifacts and records of cultural, artistic and historical value to the Kwagu't people.

The U'Mista Cultural Centre is not a static museum, but rather a focal point for the community of Natives in Alert

Bay and beyond. Its exhibits capture the struggles and mis-understandings between the Canadian government and the lifeblood of the Natives. An important example of the conflict between Natives in Canada and the Canadian government is that certain Native ceremonies were banned by law. For example, the potlatch was used by Natives to mark important occasions: the naming of children, marriage, mourning the dead, and transfering rights and privileges. The potlatch was critical to the Natives, but it was banned by the government in Canada, and also by the U.S. government for Natives who practiced this important ceremony in Alaska. The apparent purpose of the law banning the potlatch, which was enacted in 1884, was to "civilize" Natives and turn them away from Indian practices. The term "assimilation" was given to describe the policy as enacted in law both in the United States and in Canada for "civilizing" Natives. The policy in practice included removing children from their parents and raising them in boarding schools, prohibiting the use of Native languages, banning the practices of Native ceremonies—such as the potlatch—and confiscating traditional ceremonial artifacts.

A major example of outright persecution of Natives occurred in Alert Bay in December 1921. Natives held a potlatch, against government regulations. The ceremony was interrupted by the Indian agent in Alert Bay, William Halliday, and a number of police. Twenty Natives were sent to prison for up to three months; they were charged and convicted of such crimes as making speeches, dancing, and giving gifts. In addition, many artifacts used by the Natives in their ceremonies were confiscated; some were presented to museums.

In Canada the law prohibiting the potlatch was rescinded in 1951; however, the impact remains and should be remembered by all of us. The history of white and Native contacts should not be noted just in history textbooks; those of us who have the privilege of traveling along the great Inside Passage have an opportunity to be aware and remember the deeply embedded cultural assumptions and the destructive policies that followed from them.

The first curator of U'Mista Cultural Centre was Gloria Cranmer Webster, who is the granddaughter of George Hunt. Hunt was a Native who collaborated over a number of years with the anthropologist Franz Boas (during the late 1800s and early 1900s) and taught him the Kwak'wala language, for which Boas then created a written language. Hunt and Boas also carefully recorded traditional customs and ceremonies so that all were in a written language form before government laws prohibited their practice.

Port Hardy

Port Hardy, located near the northern end of Vancouver Island, is the last place to obtain fuel and provisions before crossing the open waters of Queen Charlotte Sound and then continuing north on the Inside Passage. Port Hardy is geared to handle commercial vessels, and a number of boaters feel that Port McNeill (about 20 miles to the east) is more accommodating to cruising boats whose skippers are not in the business of commercial fishing. I prefer Port Hardy because it is closer to the crossing of open water that begins the next leg of the trip. When I arrive at Port Hardy, I check in with the Harbor Master, secure a moorage spot, and begin to prepare for the next leg of the trip.

Suggestions on how to prepare for the open-ocean crossing of Queen Charlotte Sound and continuing north on the Inside Passage:

1. Obtain Provisions. Aside from two small Native villages (New Bella Bella and Klemtu), there are no towns, villages or communities or places to obtain fuel or provisions between Port Hardy and Prince Rupert—a distance of 270 nautical miles.

2. Gather Information. Check the weather forecast for information about expected winds, wave conditions, and prospects for fog or rain. Review tide charts to plan for optimal times and a range of satisfactory times to leave port.

3. Do Some Charting. Review the navigational charts that cover the area from Port Hardy to Safety Cove on Calvert Island and on up Fitz Hugh Sound. Establish way points in latitude and longitude from Port Hardy to Safety Cove, an area beyond the open-ocean crossing. This navigational information provides security in case of fog. As an example, I have a way point for harbor entrance (three miles from harbor), entrance to God's Pocket (six miles from harbor entrance), exit from God's Pocket (three miles from entrance), and corresponding way points to areas just west of Pine Island, Storm Island, Egg Island, and to a way point just east of Safety Cove. I am comfortable in making this open-ocean voyage in fog, and I have done so three times. I will not start the trip if in addition to fog there are also bad seas or a combination of moderate seas and an ebbing tide. The global positioning system (GPS) and navigational charts make it possible to follow an appropriate route under conditions of poor visibility.

4. Spend Talk Time. Take time to walk up and down the docks and talk to boaters who have just made the trip from the other direction or who plan to make the trip under the first "right conditions." Often I will share call

signals and agree either to leave at about the same time or at least to communicate along the way. With all this done I am ready.

Leg III:
Port Hardy to Prince Rupert
(approximate distance 277 miles)

Crossing Queen Charlotte Sound
(approximate distance 75 miles):
Port Hardy to Safety Cove

In the portion of this passage that is open to the ocean, there are three conditions of concern: tide and current, wind and waves, and fog. Of those three you can eliminate the first as a source of difficulty by reviewing your tide book and planning to leave port at such a time that at least the open ocean portion of the trip is made during an incoming- or flood-tide condition. One of the problems of being in Queen Charlotte Sound during an ebb tide condition is that strong currents will pour out of the large inlets, such as Rivers Inlet, and create especially difficult and confused seas. The second potential concern (wind and waves) is substantially mitigated by the high quality of information that is available from Alert Bay's continuous weather broadcast. What is especially useful are reports of current conditions from the lighthouse keeper at Egg Island. This information can help you make a go or a no-go decision before leaving port.

A word about fog. Fog at sea used to bother me a lot. In fact, I would say that, next to being on a sinking boat, not knowing where I was while at sea was my most unpleasant, gut-wrenching, white-knuckle type of experience.

However, it began to dawn on me that it wasn't the fog that bothered me as much as not knowing where I was. Based on my experience I now reduce my fears and anxiety about being lost while attempting this—or other—passages by establishing course lines, taking compass readings and measuring distances between way points. While underway I keep track of boat speed and time (especially times when way points are reached), and I make regular entries in my log. I use a GPS to add a reality test by its continuous monitoring and reporting of position in latitude and longitude. I have made the trip under conditions of fog, but I have not had an unpleasant crossing. With these very standard precautions I have been able to make the crossing in a normal amount of time for my vessel. Averaging about 15 knots, it takes between four and five hours to go from Port Hardy to Safety Cove, an area sheltered by Calvert Island. A boat traveling five knots per hour may take three times that long.

Pruth Bay on Calvert Island

About seven miles north of Safety Cove is Kwakshua Channel, which lies between Calvert Island and Hecate Island. About five miles into Kwakshua Channel is Pruth Bay and an excellent anchorage. My wife and I took that side trip in 1995, and anchored about one-quarter mile from the west end of the bay. We launched our dinghy, rowed to shore, and walked around the grounds and buildings of the Hakai Beach Resort. The resort offers lodging, meals, boats and guides who take guests on fishing trips in nearby waters for salmon and halibut. What we especially enjoyed was the short hike from the beach at Pruth Bay to the beach on the west side of Calvert Island. The beach is strewn with logs beached from heavy winter storms, and small islands dot the view just offshore. The Pacific Ocean west of Calvert Island is open ocean and the land at the same latitude (52) to the west is Siberia. Pruth Bay is very well protected; it must be fun to be there in safety during a storm when just a mile to the west the Pacific is roiling.

Namu

In early June, 1997, Dick Ecklund, a retired engineer from North Carolina, and I were making this trip and had just come across the sound from Port Hardy in the fog. Once we approached Calvert Island, we left the fog behind us and enjoyed sunny skies and mild temperatures. Moving north through Fitz Hugh Sound, we came across several Dall porpoises. They swam right up to us and made multiple leaps along the waves created by the bow of our boat. They turned at will, jumping freely and at tremendous speeds, which I estimated at about 25 to 30 knots. They must have thought we were slow indeed. Dall porpoises are the only mammals in the whale group that actively play with a boat and with the waves coming either off the bow or off the stern. Good numbers of them are seen along the Canadian portion of the Inside Passage.

As we continued on our way we decided to go to Namu, park the boat, hike and explore the town. Namu is about 20 miles north of Safety Cove, just off the eastern shore of Fitz Hugh Sound. It is situated so close to the main route of the Inside Passage that it is not out of the way should one stop there. As Dick and I slowly approached this town by boat, we were struck by how pretty it looked from a distance. We could see a large building (the cannery) on the northwest section of "town" and attractive white-painted houses dotting the hillside. We saw what looked like a dormitory and a number of other large buildings.

We tied up our boat to a float east of the cannery building and met a man at the company dock who introduced himself as the caretaker and the sole resident of Namu. He said we were free to walk around, take pictures and ask questions. Dick and I walked up the ramp and looked through a window of the company store, still stocked with food although it had not been open for years. We visited a warehouse that housed seven large diesel-powered generators that once supplied electricity for the town and the substantial power needs of the cannery. While we were there, Jack Cabena, the caretaker activated one engine for maintenance purposes. All of the generators were in operating condition. We hiked to a large lake one mile southeast of the town and admired the pipes, constructed of wood, that supplied the substantial water needs of the cannery and people who once lived at Namu.

Two First Nation Natives recall a past and vibrant Namu

As we hiked back from the lake to town, we noticed two men approaching in an outboard-powered, open, aluminum boat. They ran their boat almost to shore in front of the large building that looked like a dorm. When they stopped they were only about 30 feet from where Dick and I were standing. I knew they likely did not come from Port Hardy in their type of boat, and the only town nearby was the town of New Bella Bella—a First Nation village—about 15 miles northwest of Namu.

I asked if they were fishing.

"No," said the boat operator, "just looking."

I asked if they could tell me about Namu. Not a word.

"Are you familiar with the name Boas?" I asked.
"Do you mean Franz Boas, the anthropologist?" one asked. I nodded yes. Both men had read three of the books written by Boas and thought they were pretty good.

Franz Boas was an anthropologist who spent much time in the late 1800s studying Native cultures in British Columbia. He was intrigued by the successful adaptation of Northwest Indians to their environment and thought that they were an example of the diversity of human adaptation and showed the range of human possibilities. He learned the language of Kwakiutl Natives and studied their culture, religious beliefs and ceremonies. He was very concerned about the relentless pressures placed on these Indians to forsake their traditions and language and adopt European customs and the English language. He helped to acquit some Natives who had been arrested for participating in Native ceremonies that had been banned in British Columbia. His work is remembered by many Natives in British Columbia

Local Natives describe their experiences working in Namu between 1960 and 1975.

and Alaska. The diversion into the work of Boas broke the ice. The man operating the boat said, "Let me tell you about Namu."

He went on to say that he and his friend had worked at Namu for about 15 years, through the 1960s and up until the cannery closed in about 1976. He told us there were

This was the housing for the Chinese workers at the cannery.

three kinds of workers and they were separated by where they lived. Natives from the area were housed in the large buildings to the right, and the Chinese laborers were housed in the large dorm building in front of us. The whites who managed the place as foremen, supervisors, and mechanics and the maintenance workers lived in the individual houses. The main boss lived in the large house in front of the sea-plane float. The Chinese worked in the canneries after the work on the railroad was completed. "They were paid Chinese wages," he said, laughing at that. "Some of us (Natives) fished with company boats and delivered the fish to the cannery. We were paid 30 cents a fish, regardless of the size. Others of us worked in the cannery, including a lot of Native women."

The man paused and then said: "Then this cannery shut down; in fact, the only canneries still operating are at Prince Rupert [northernmost city in B.C.] or at Vancouver [the southernmost city in B.C.]. All the canneries in central B.C. are shut down. That is too bad for us. At one time about 39 percent of the commercial catch in B.C. was made by Natives; now it is down to about 2 percent. Many Natives worked in the canneries like this one, but all of those workers lost their jobs and are on welfare."

I asked him why the cannery had been shut down and why the Natives were now almost completely out of the business of salmon fishing and fish processing. He paused for a while and must have remembered how our conversation had started. He said what happened, including government policy and the business decisions made by B.C. Packing Company, was a matter of record. "Look it up," he suggested, then offered, "and if you have any questions give me a call." He gave me his name, phone number and fax number. We had gone full circle. At the start I asked him about Boas, and he had already done his homework. Now, when I asked about Native fishing and their work at the canneries, it was my turn to do some reading and homework.

First canneries after contact

The first cannery on the Fraser River was opened in 1871. The technology for commercial canning had been developed in Europe some 50 years earlier. The tin for the canning was imported from England, and most of the canned salmon was shipped, around the Horn, to Great Britain. A few hundred cases were canned in 1871; ten years later that number increased to 142,516 cases. The majority of the salmon were caught by Native fishermen, who manned company-owned gill-net boats. Other Native men, Native women, and Chinese laborers worked in the canneries—sometimes 18 hours a day. At the end of the season the workers settled accounts with the company store and went home with whatever earnings were left over.

Native fishing restrictions

The canning operations grew in number and eventually covered the entire British Columbia coastline from Vancouver in the south to Prince Rupert in the north. In 1904, cannery operators convinced government officials in Ottawa that if the Natives on the Skeena River did not stop their salmon fishing, the canning industry (on the Skeena) would be destroyed. Hans Helgesen, a fisheries overseer, was sent by the Canadian government to inform the chief of the Babine Indians that their fish traps on the Skeena River were illegal and must be removed. He also told the chief that it was illegal for Indians to sell fish independent of the canneries, and that they must have a permit to catch fish for food, known as subsistence fishing. Natives could fish only out of company-owned boats and deliver their catch to the canneries, and they could work in the canneries. Other fishing done by Natives was viewed as poaching. This policy of severe restrictions on Native fishing became law throughout British Columbia.

Natives given the right to own and operate fishing boats

Not until 1942 were Natives in B.C. given the right to purchase and own commercial fishing vessels; Sames Sewid, a Kwakiutl seine fisherman, was the first Native in

B.C. to own his own boat as an independent fisherman. He sold his catch to canneries. Eventually many Natives were able to build or purchase a vessel for commercial fishing. The great majority of them caught comparatively small numbers of salmon, but their catch—and their earnings—were important to them.

The Davis Plan

On September 8, 1968, Jack Davis, the Canadian fisheries minister, announced a plan to limit licenses of commercial fishing vessels. Under the assertion that there were too many boats and fishermen chasing too few fish, he announced a plan that drastically changed salmon fishing in B.C. He announced a two-tier vessel license program. Highly productive fishermen—those who had landed 10,000 pounds or more in the years of 1967 or 1968—would be given an "A" license. Those who had caught less than 10,000 pounds were given a "B" license. The "B" licenses were set to expire in ten years. Companies that owned a large number of small fishing boats rented to fishermen could trade in the "B" permits, canceling out the smaller vessels, and obtain "A" permits, then build new, large, efficient and fast commercial fishing boats. Hundreds of small boats were eliminated under this policy and replaced with a smaller number of vessels with vastly increased catching power.

This single government act enabled the owners of large canneries to shut down all the canneries in central British Columbia. The new commercial fishing boats had both large capacity and modern refrigeration, and they were fast. They could stay on the fishing grounds until their fish holds were full, and then take their catch to canneries and fish processing plants in either Prince Rupert or Vancouver. By 1969, more than a thousand shore workers—mostly Natives—lost their jobs. More losses followed. The great majority of Natives who had acquired their own boats were given "B" licenses, which expired in 1979. The current status of Native participation in salmon fisheries in British Columbia is lower now than at any point since the time of first contact.

Silence in the central-B.C. portion of the Inside Passage

As Dick and I returned to our boat to head up the remainder of Fitz Hugh Sound on our way to New Bella Bella, I was reminded again that the most striking aspect of the Canadian Inside Passage, once one leaves Vancouver Island, is the isolation and remoteness. Fewer people live on the coastal section of this vast but remote part of British Columbia than earlier in this century. The canneries (with Namu as just one example) are shut down, the logging companies so heavily mechanized that they employ far fewer workers than before. Logging camps that once dotted the area are now gone, and with them dreams of stable employment and viable communities. Ocean Falls, at the end of Fisher Channel, is now inhabited by a remnant of people who use the former mill town as a yacht club and vacation or retirement residence. Other logging camps are now overgrown with vegetation and remain as silent ghost towns hidden from view. The terrain is too steep for agriculture, and the land is so fractured by long, deep fjords that road-building is not feasible. For some the silence is disquieting and foreboding, but for me the entire portion of the Inside Passage is outstanding in its beauty, including this most remote and long section. The only way to appreciate it is by boat.

New Bella Bella

From Namu we proceeded north into Fisher Channel, and just past Fog Rocks we turned to the west at Kaiete Point and into Lama Passage to the First Nation town of New Bella Bella. Fuel is available and the public docks offer moorage for transient vessels at no charge. Across Lama Passage from New Bella Bella is Shearwater, a fishing and diving resort, with a hotel, restaurant, showers, fuel and moorage.

Greenpeace is frequently present in New Bella Bella. I spoke with Catherine Stewart of Greenpeace in Canada. She explained that Greenpeace is attempting to alert Canadians to the destructive clearcutting logging practices that have essentially removed all old-growth timber in British Columbia, with little regard for providing buffers near streams and rivers or steep slopes.

Dick and I spoke briefly with five members of Greenpeace who had just returned to New Bella Bella after having chained themselves to a yarder to halt logging in a nearby timber harvest area. A motto of Greenpeace is that industrial practices that are destructive to the environment will not occur without witness or protest; the group of five— three women and two men— had spent five days and nights in the outdoors to make their protest.

Klemtu

Klemtu is another Native village, about 40 miles from New Bella Bella. The boat trip from New Bella Bella is very attractive. Two miles north of New Bella Bella a lighthouse marks the entrance to Seaforth Channel. Thirteen miles along that channel, we arrived at Ivory Island and the entrance to Milbanke Sound. Milbanke Sound is open to swells from the north Pacific, and if the conditions are hazardous, it is wise to avoid it and follow the more protected route of Reid Channel, which leads to Jackson Passage and cuts west to Finlayson Channel. Klemtu in situated on Swindle Island, just west of Finlayson Channel. The small harbor is extremely well protected, with Cone Island only 200 yards to the east, separated from Swindle Island by a narrow but deep channel. Klemtu once had a cannery, but it closed with scores of others in 1969.

The Anglican Church at Klemtu

In July of 1996, I pulled into Klemtu on a Sunday afternoon, fueled up and decided to stay at Klemtu overnight. I parked the boat within the inner harbor and walked through the small town. I noticed an Anglican Church about two blocks from the south part of the harbor. A sign indicated the evening service would begin at 7 p.m. I returned to my boat, fixed a dinner, and around 6:30 p.m. heard church music being broadcast from speakers attached to the outside of the church. I decided to attend the service, so I left the boat, walked to the church and arrived in front of the open doors just before the scheduled starting time of seven. I looked inside and saw that there were no members present. A minister stood in front of the church by the pulpit. A woman, probably his wife, was also standing in front. There was no one else in church, and no one was walking towards the church. I decided to cancel my church attendance plans and walked away from the entrance and back towards my boat. I passed two Native men sitting on a bench along the boardwalk which borders the west side of the bay. I stopped to talk with them and asked if local Natives attend the church.

"No," one of the men said. "We elders believe it is very important for the young people to learn about our history, our language and our customs. If you want to see something, go over to the dock on the other side of this bay. There you will see a canoe, about 40 feet long, that was built by a master canoe-builder with the help of seven young men from our Native village of Klemtu. The master canoe-builder is from Kitimat; his father was a master canoe-builder, as was his grandfather. He learned the art of canoe-building from them and he is passing on his knowledge and expert craftsmanship to some of our young men. This is very important to us and we are very proud. Next year some tribal leaders will paddle that sea-going canoe through the Inside Passage to Victoria and then to Neah Bay on the coast of Washington. This was a very traditional

Large Native dugout canoe.

voyage for our people in the past, and we want to repeat this trip at least once every four years."

I walked over to look at the canoe. I was stunned by the high quality of the workmanship. It was made out of one very large cedar log, with slats of hewn boards set as seats to provide for a crew of about 12. This was a reminder to me of a renewal in British Columbia, as well as in Southeast Alaska, of Native culture as seen through a resurgence of interest in art, woodwork, Native language usage and ceremonies. I interpret the absence of church attendance in Klemtu, and a resurgence of interest in canoe-building and other traditional activities of Native culture, as a statement of noncompliance and rejection of those who had urged and coerced the indigenous people to abandon Native ways and adopt an exclusive adherence to European-American language, customs and religious beliefs.

The small Native community of Klemtu is the last inhabited village along the Canadian Inside Passage until one arrives in Prince Rupert, about 140 miles away. The passage from this point on is a continuation of a natural marine water route that is narrow and deep and protected by steep coastal mountains on the mainland side and steep hills on the islands that separate the passage from the Pacific. The deepest part of the entire Alaskan-Canadian Inside Passage is in Finlayson Channel, just east of Swindle Island and Klemtu. The depth reaches an astonishing 418 fathoms (2508 feet).

Princess Royal Island: Home of elusive white bears and an abandoned company town.

Forty miles north of Klemtu, tucked into a small bay on the east side of Princess Royal Island, is the abandoned cannery town of Butedale, once operated by the Canadian Fishing Company but closed in 1969 as part of the massive reorganization of commercial fish processing in B.C. following the enactment of the Davis Plan. A large waterfall thunders down on the east side of the abandoned town. The cannery was purchased a few years ago by several Oregon families who plan to rebuild the derelict docks and some of the buildings and establish a business selling fuel and supplies to boaters and fishermen who travel past.

My son Paul and I spent two days at Butedale in June of 1995; we hiked to a large lake about a half mile from Butedale and walked through the rain forest. We hoped to spot some white bears, which, though rare, are more prevalent on Princess Royal Island than anywhere else. These white bears are in fact black bears with white fur. The name is Ursus Americanus Kermodei, which was designated by the naturalist William Hornaday in 1904. There is speculation that these bears have white fur due to adaptation during the Ice Age and that the trait continues. White fur (among black bears) is a recessive trait, so that both male and female bears must carry the gene for an offspring to express the trait. In Canada these bears are protected by law. Paul and I did not have the luck of seeing any of these bears, although we did see some deer. We very much enjoyed the opportunity for a hike and appreciated having even the chance to see a bear in the wild. Later on our journey we had the opportunity to see bears as well as other wildlife. We met and spoke with Mark Clark and Lee and Mitch Strong (Oregonians who now are among the owners of Butedale) and talked with them about their hopes and plans to revive a piece of Butedale in this remote, isolated, but historic and attractive setting.

Bishop Bay Hot Springs

About 12 miles north of Butedale is the end of Princess Royal Island and the beginning of McKay Reach, which begins the last stretch of the passage to Prince Rupert. However, just eight miles north of the entrance to McKay Reach is Bishop Bay and its famous hot springs. Local people from Kitimat have built an enclosed and covered pool, which is fed by a continuous flow of hot spring water. The area is user-maintained and is well worth a stop and a lengthy, refreshing bath. A 70-foot float provides moorage at no charge.

Public dock at Bishop Bay Hot Springs.

Grenville Channel

From Bishop Bay one must backtrack to McKay Reach, cross Wright Sound and enter Grenville Channel. This channel is the narrowest and straightest part of the Inside Passage. The channel is 45 miles long, and on the mainland side there are several excellent inlets providing good anchorage, including Lowe Inlet, Klewnuggit Inlet, Baker Inlet, and West Inlet. Grenville Channel ends at the mouth or delta of the Skeena River, which is second to the Fraser River in terms of its importance to the commercial salmon industry in B.C. Kennedy Island straddles the delta area of the Skeena and is only 20 miles south of Prince Rupert. I expect fog when I reach this area, and I usually find it. I learned the first time through the importance of having way points clearly designated, routes established with compass headings and positions in latitude and longitude charted to track with our GPS. The first time through this area, I was with my son Paul and we hit very heavy fog in the area of Kennedy Island. I carefully positioned the boat near the is-land, while Paul pulled out the charts and began the task of planning our route from that point to the harbor at Prince Rupert. We put all the way points and positions figures in our log, so I have them for future reference, but I should have completed that task while docked at warm, sunny Bishop Bay.

Prince Rupert

Prince Rupert, the "gateway to Alaska" city, was estab-lished in 1905 as the terminus of Canada's second trans-continental railroad—the Canadian National Railroad. The city is situated on Kaien Island and was founded by a U.S. citizen, Charles Hayes, who recognized the potential as a world-class port and transportation center. The city received its name in 1906 as a result of a contest sponsored by the Grand Trunk Pacific Railway. The company offered a prize of $250 for the best name for the city. Ms. Eleanor MacDonald won the prize with the suggestion of Prince Rupert, named after the first governor of the Hudson Bay Company. The railroad was completed in 1914 at a cost comparable to the construction cost of the Panama Canal.

Prince Rupert and the city of Vancouver represent major transportation links to the rest of Canada—and the world. With a population of about 18,000, Prince Rupert is the second largest city on the B.C. mainland coast. The only other city on the north B.C. mainland coast is Kitimat, with a population of about 12,000. The Native villages, such as New Bella Bella and Klemtu, are much smaller in population and are situated on islands, separated from the mainland by the Inside Passage.

Prince Rupert has the second deepest harbor in the world and is a major transportation center for shipping fish and timber. The northern B.C. fishing fleet is centered in Prince Rupert. The Skeena River, south of Prince Rupert, and the Nass River, north of Prince Rupert, are major salmon producers. For the boater traveling north, Prince Rupert has ample moorages, stores with provisions, and marine repair facilities. Ketchikan, Alaska, is just 90 miles away—and the border to Alaska is part way across the Dixon Entrance.

Historical and Cultural Opportunities in Prince Rupert, B.C.

Prince Rupert and surrounding areas have the largest number of Native archaeological sites in British Columbia. This is due to the fact that the area is centered amidst two important rivers—the Skeena and the Nass—which provided abundant salmon, halibut, and other foods for Natives who have lived here for over 10,000 years. Even today, the city of Prince Rupert is considered a center for highly skilled Native artists. In my view, the Museum of Northern British Columbia, the North Coast Cannery Museum, and the Ksan Historical Village offer the best highlights of First Nation and Euro-Canadian history and culture in the area around Prince Rupert.

Museum of Northern British Columbia

The Museum of Northern B.C. has long been present in Prince Rupert. However, in 1997 the museum was moved to a new and much more spacious location than before at 100 First Ave., West Prince Rupert, B.C. The museum's architecture is based on Native longhouse design, which adds to the experience of art. The museum represents a major public investment and urban renewal. More important, it provides a statement that the major art forms it displays, which are of exceptional quality, are local to the area. The museum reviews the history of Euro-Canadian settlement in Northern B.C. and provides information about the commercial fishing industry It houses a significant display of Native art, including art from Haida Indians of the Queen Charlotte Islands and from Klingit and Tsimshian peoples who live along the coast and inland in B.C.

While visiting the museum in its new facility in June 1998, I met two Native artists in residence at the museum. Mr. Lee-Am-Lachoo was busy creating a ceremonial robe to be presented and worn at an upcoming Native festival. He told me that Natives in British Columbia regard Prince Rupert as a center for the most productive and highest quality Native art. Also present at the museum was Mr. Moral Russ, who is a master sculptor of a rare stone obtained from Slate Chuck Mountain on the Queen Charlotte Islands. His work is of museum quality and many of his creations are displayed in Canada and other countries. A point to remember is that the opportunity to talk in person with Native artists greatly enhances the appreciation of viewing the art in this museum. It helps a visitor to learn the function and meaning of the art for the Natives within their culture.

North Pacific Cannery Village Museum at
Port Edward, British Columbia

The North Pacific Cannery was built in 1889 at Inverness Passage near the mouth of the Skeena River. It closed in 1972 but was declared a National Historic Site on its 100th birthday in 1989 and is open to the public as a historic museum. The location of the museum at Port Edward is only a few miles south of Prince Rupert, and one can get there by cab or by a bus from Prince Rupert. Information about the North Pacific Village Museum is available at the Museum of Northern B.C. in Prince Rupert.

British Columbia is a resource-rich Province, with timber and fish (particularly salmon) being of critical importance to the economy for Natives for thousands of years and now for Natives and Euro-Canadians since the time of contact. The salmon industry has seen vast changes not only in the amount of salmon, but also in the methods of catching the fish and in fish processing. Between the years 1864 and 1966, 250 canneries were built in British Columbia. The number of canneries is now reduced to six, and those are either in Prince Rupert or Vancouver. The modern ones now work 12 months a year and often 24 hours a day. They handle many kinds of fish in addition to salmon, as well as shrimp and crab. Most of the fish is processed and shipped either fresh or frozen. Canning is still an important part of fish processing, but not nearly to the degree it was 100 years ago.

The North Pacific Cannery is the oldest intact cannery on the B.C. coast. Many canneries—such as the one at Butedale, B.C.—were built on pilings, and the structures are rotting and falling into the sea. The fact that so many abandoned canneries are in decay adds to the importance of keeping at least one such cannery intact and open to the public for a better understanding and appreciation of our past. David Boyce, a heritage interpreter and educator, is the museum progammer for North Pacific Cannery Village Museum. He is an excellent resource for an overview of past and current information about the salmon industry in British Columbia, as well as how the first canneries (such as the North Pacific Cannery) processed fish, and how the work force of Chinese and Japanese, First Nation peoples, and Euro-Canadians who owned and managed the canneries lived and worked in a highly segregated manner to catch, process, and sometimes deplete the resource.

Ksan Historical Village, Hazelton, British Columbia

The Ksan Historical Village is located at the junction of the Skeena and Bulkley Rivers. For thousands of years, this area was the home of Gitksan and Wet' suewe' ten Indian peoples. They share a common linguistic root with the Tsimshian people from the mouth of the Skeena. The Ksan Historical Village is not along the Inside Passage; it is 180 miles east of Prince Rupert (288 kilometres). Rail and bus service is available from Prince Rupert, or one can drive along Highway 16. Each option follows the scenic Skeena River.

The Ksan Historical Village contains totem poles and seven reconstructed longhouses, each with a capacity to house a clan or a group of many families who were descended from a common ancestor. Longhouses are magnificant structures, built of planks from large cedar trees and with a central area for a fire pit and one hole in the roof for the smoke to exit. This village shows how First Nation peoples lived prior to first contact—and after. One longhouse (The Frog House of the Distant Past) is furnished in the manner prior to white contact. Another is furnished as if in preparation for a potlatch. Three longhouses are used as a museum, a gift shop with a book store, and a carving school. Over the centuries First Nation peoples spent considerable time as artists crafting ceremonial masks, totem poles, wall panels and jewelry. This tradition continues at Ksan and visitors can view artists creating works at the House of Wood Carving. Young Native artists are taught these skills to ensure the preservation of artifacts and ancient ways and to breathe new life into a tradition of First Nation creativity so their art will contine to develop and not remain static.

Unresolved problems facing the peoples of British Columbia

As I have traveled through the waters of the Inside Passage in British Columbia, visiting both the cities and the Native villages, it is unmistakable that two important unresolved problems are of serious concern to the citizens of British Columbia: the U.S.-Canada salmon dispute, and unresolved First Nation claims against the Canadian government and the Province of British Columbia. I dwell on these issues and comment on them because both problems affect U.S. citizens as well. Those of us who travel the Inside Passage can hardly escape hearing about these concerns.

The U.S. - Canada Salmon Conflict

In recent years a person traveling by private boat through British Columbia received clear information about an ongoing and unresolved conflict between British Columbia and the United States over salmon harvesting. Marine radio transmissions were frequently interrupted with a "Notice to Mariners" broadcast. The broadcast informed all operators of foreign commercial fishing vessels to notify the Canadian Coast Guard upon arrival in Canadian waters. Their vessels could then be inspected. Failure to report could result in forfeiture of vessel, imprisonment and fine. Newspapers in British Columbia gave daily reports about the lack of progress in coming to an agreement with Alaska over fishing quotas and the problem of the high rate of interception of Canada-bound fish by Alaskan fishermen. While this problem goes back many years, the intensity of the conflict is heightened in recent years. In July of 1995, a fisherman who stepped off an Alaskan fishing vessel in Prince Rupert, B.C., was assaulted and killed by seven young men. The tragedy was compounded by irony; the victim was a Canadian citizen who was employed on an Alaskan fishing boat. It was like a Greek tragedy in which a woman imagines herself a hero after killing an "evil" man, later to find the man she killed was her son.

Also, in July of 1997, hundreds of commercial fishermen in Prince Rupert used their fishing boats to block an Alaskan ferry boat for three days. While I was in Prince Rupert in 1997, court hearings were underway to determine the penalty for a Seattle-based fisherman charged with "failing to report" after entering British Columbia waters.

None of this conflict spreads over to recreational boaters from the U.S. while cruising through British Columbia. I mention the conflict because it is very important news in B.C., and for that reason should be of interest to those of us who travel through the scenic waters of British Columbia.

A perspective on the salmon conflict:

As long ago as 1885, commercial fishermen in the state of Washington and fishermen in British Columbia knew that Fraser River-bound sockeye salmon on the homeward migration came through the Strait of Juan de Fuca and swam close to the Washington coastline before turning north to enter the Fraser River. Washington fishermen regularly intercepted these fish. In the north along the U.S.-Canada border, sockeye salmon as well as huge runs of pink and chum salmon commingle on both sides of latitude 54.40. Essentially, all of the sockeye salmon caught in this border area between the two countries originate in two Canadian rivers—the Nass and the Skeena.

The U. S. and Canada reached an agreement in 1985 called the U.S.-Canada Salmon Treaty, but the treaty broke down in 1992 and the conflict remains unresolved. One major sticking point is that Canada wants to limit the interception by U.S. fishermen of Canada-bound sockeye salmon headed for the Nass and the Skeena Rivers to 120,000 fish. U. S. fishermen insist that the quota be flexible so that in years of high abundance the allowed interception would be higher. Charlie Wentland, a salmon fisherman from Wrangell, Alaska, told me that the number of Canada-bound fish caught by Alaskan fishermen represents less than 2 percent of the total Alaskan salmon catch. That number seems pretty close because the salmon catch in Alaska exceeds 100 million fish. He went on to say that if commercial fishermen in Alaska stop fishing in Alaskan waters to avoid a comparatively small catch of Canada-bound fish, a tremendous opportunity would be lost. On the other hand, commercial fishermen (salmon fishermen) in British Columbia are facing economic ruin, and much of the problem is now focussed in the area of Prince Rupert. Canadians have told me they are insulted when told that the Alaskan interception of Canadian fish is only a small portion of the vast numbers of fish caught by Alaskan fishermen and angered that their threatened salmon are harvested at will by U.S. fishermen.

The issue is important and a solution must be created; there is no easy or pat answer. The overriding issue is that the United States and Canada must develop a cooperative treaty that protects wild fish and permits sustainable fisheries.

Building a Better Relationship Between Aboriginal and Non-Aboriginal Canadians: Gathering Strength

In January 1998, Jane Stewart, Minister of Indian Affairs and Northern Development, initiated what many hope will form a new era in the relationship between Aboriginal and non-Aboriginal Canadians. She announced the creation of the Gathering Strength—Canada's Aboriginal Action Plan, which calls for 1) recognizing past mistakes and injustices, 2) commencing reconciliation, and 3) rebuilding on strengths and successes.

Reconciliation and expression of regret

Coinciding with the announcement of Gathering Strength, the Government of Canada offered a Statement of Reconciliation to aboriginal people in Canada. A portion of this Statement of Reconciliation says:

"As Aboriginal and non-Aboriginal Canadians seek to move forward together in a process of renewal, it is essential that we deal with the legacies of the past affecting the Aboriginal peoples of Canada. ... Our purpose is not to rewrite history, but, rather to learn from our past and to find ways to deal with the negative impacts that certain historical decisions continue to have in our society today.

"Sadly, our history with respect to the treatment of Aboriginal people is not something in which we can take pride. ... As a country, we are burdened by past actions that resulted in weakening the identity of Aboriginal people, suppressing their language and cultures, and outlawing spiritual practices. ... The Government of Canada today formally expresses to all Aboriginal people in Canada our profound regret for past actions of the federal government which have contributed to these difficult pages in the history of our relationship together."

Next Steps

Four major objectives of Gathering Strength are:

(1) Renewing the partnerships between Aboriginal and non-Aboriginal Canadians through treaty negotiations;
(2) Strengthening Aboriginal Governance. In B.C. this would occur as part of the treaty process;
(3) Developing a new fiscal relationship with a goal of fiscal autonomy;
(4) Supporting strong communities, people and economies.

Nisga'a Indians Sign Historic Treaty

On August 4, 1998, Nisga'a Indians in Nass Valley signed a historic treaty giving them land, cash and self-government. Because the treaty will likely establish a pattern for perhaps 50 more Indian communities in British Columbia, this treaty is important and historic.

First Nation peoples in British Columbia did not sign treaties during the period of colonization; in contrast, the rest of Canada's Aboriginal peoples did sign treaties. Prior to the Nisga'a signing, no treaty had been signed in British Columbia this century.

The Nisga'a Indians had persisted for well over a hundred years in demanding title to land that they had lived on for thousands of years prior to white contact and subsequent colonization. As far back as 1885, a Nisga'a Indian named Neis Puck challenged members of a Royal Commission of Inquiry. He questioned the authority that took Indian land and gave it to the Crown, saying, "Who is the chief that gave this land to the Queen? Give us his name, we have never heard of him."

Indian Act of 1927 suppresses Indian land claims

In response to persistent protests of First Nation peoples against British Columbia and the federal government over their rights, the Canadian government passed a law which prohibited lawyers from assisting Indians in pursuing land claims. Section 141 of the 1927 version of the Indian Act provided for up to a two-month prison sentence for any person who assisted a tribe or band of Indians for the recovery of any claim.

In the context of the Indian Act of 1927, it is easy to understand why no treaty was signed for many decades by First Nation peoples in British Columbia. While times have changed, many actions by both industry and government gave little room for hope for First Nation peoples. Such actions include the Davis Plan of the 1960s that had the effect of reducing Native participation in the salmon industry, and government allocation of rights to harvest timber on land claimed by First Nation peoples.

What are the benefits to the Nisga'a Indians?

They will receive $126 million in cash over 15 years and title to 745 square miles in rugged, resource-rich northwestern British Columbia. The treaty is also important to non-Aboriginal Canadian citizens. This treaty will end uncertainty faced by timber companies and mining companies as they consider new projects on land now under the control by the Nisga'a Indians.

As a U.S. citizen, I am impressed with the scope of the work that led up to Gathering Strength and the frankness of the apology made by the Canadian government. U.S. citizens may well want to consider these actions in Canada.

Northwest to Alaska: Southeast Alaska and the Alaskan Inside Passage

Crossing the Dixon Entrance: Prince Rupert to Ketchikan

The distance from Prince Rupert to Ketchikan, Alaska, is about 90 miles, and it includes an open-ocean crossing—the Dixon Entrance—of about 30 miles. In 1995, on my first trip to Alaska with Second Effort, I was anxious about the crossing and remained for a few days at the Prince Rupert Yacht Club. My friend, Eric Mash, who planned to meet me in Ketchikan, already had arrived there and was waiting my arrival. Because of my delay in leaving Prince Rupert, Eric flew from Ketchikan on a small float plane and met me in Prince Rupert. The next day we left the harbor and traveled through the well-marked Venn Passage into Chatham Sound and headed north towards Dundas Island, which is about one-third of the way to Ketchikan. The trip was so uneventful that I felt I had been overly cautious for having waited extra days in Prince Rupert. We did see a pod of about ten Orca whales—which were dramatic—but no bad seas.

It is, however, prudent to allocate for some days of "no go" because of weather conditions, and all boaters I have spoken to plan for that. A boater may have to hold up in port for a day or two at either Port Hardy (entrance to Queen Charlotte Sound—and an open-ocean crossing) or at Prince

Rupert (Dixon Entrance) on the way north to wait out weather. The same strategy would hold for a return trip south, with the possibility of a wait in Ketchikan for a return to Prince Rupert, or a wait in Safety Cove off Calvert Island before heading to Port Hardy.

With good weather on arrival at Dundas Island, Eric and I proceeded north and checked our charts and the GPS to determine when we reached latitude 54:40—the boundary between Alaska and Canada. Had the weather and sea conditions turned difficult, we would have sought anchorage at Dundas Island.

As we entered Alaskan waters, we admired the heavily forested coastal range to the east, which marks the southern boundary of the Misty Fjord National Monument. Proceeding north past Foggy Bay (part of Misty Fjord to our east), we passed Duke Island and Mary Island—to our west—and entered Revillagigedo Channel and headed on into Ketchikan.

Ketchikan

Ketchikan is the first port-of-call for northbound ships coming into Alaska from the south. It has a population of 8,557 (ADCRA, 1995), with 15 percent being Native. The area was an important summer fishing area for Tlingit Indians, but outsiders were attracted to the area because of the abundance of fish and timber. Gold brought a large number of miners to the area in the 1890s and Gold Creek Street remains as a tourist attraction to commemorate a way of life that was vibrant a hundred years ago. Ketchikan is a major stopover for cruise ships, drawing over 500,000 visitors per year by cruise ship alone.

The Southeast Alaska Visitor Center (50 Main Street, Ketchikan, Alaska 99901) provides an excellent overview of Southeast Alaska in terms of history, Native culture, and timber and fishery resources. Especially impressive are the exhibits concerning current issues in S.E. Alaska. For example, in 1997 the forestry exhibit showing management practices within the Tongass National Forest had displays asserting that the cutting of timber in S.E. Alaska must follow guidelines pertaining to steepness of slope, proximity to streams, and soil stability to reduce harmful impact on fish and wildlife habitat. The display then showed that the Ketchikan Pulp Mill, which began operation in 1954 and was a major employer, was shut down on March 25, 1997. When I asked about the mill closure, the woman at the information desk explained how to obtain a complete copy (six volumes) of the Tongass Land Management Plan Revision, 1997.

The visitor center also provides information about the Misty Fjord National Monument and can make reservations for visitors to rent forest cabins, as well as dispense information and maps about hiking trails.

Across the street from the visitor center is The Tongass Historical Museum, which provides insight into Native culture and S.E. Alaska history. These exhibits explain the laws, social structure and different languages of the various tribes (before time of contact), as well as common features in their practices of hunting, gathering and preserving foods. Food supplies in the forms of fish, game, berries, roots and others were so abundant that members of tribes had ample time to perfect distinctive and unique art forms and to teach their children values and cultural practices.

Another interesting activity is to visit the Totem Heritage Center, which houses 33 totem poles salvaged from abandoned Tlingit and Haida villages.

Misty Fjords National Monument

The Misty Fjords National Monument is vast in size, consisting of 2,294,343 acres situated in the southern end of Southeast Alaska. The area was created as a national monument in 1978 by presidential proclamation. The Alaska National Interest Lands Conservation Act (ANILCA) in 1980 reconfirmed the national monument classification and designated most of the monument as wilderness, but withheld 156,210 acres as nonwilderness. The nonwilderness portion received that designation in order to accommodate the mining of the Quartz Hill molybdenum deposit. The southern part of the monument is bordered with Canada by the Portland Canal, a deep, 75-mile long fjord. The monument straddles Behm Canal, another deep fjord, and includes part of the eastern side of Revillagigedo Island. The northeast section of the monument is bordered by a mountain ridge separating British Columbia from the U.S.

Misty Fjords is a pristine wilderness setting, and the designation as a national monument preserves the unique geologic and plant and animal life. The timber is old growth and remains off-limits to timber harvest. Prior to the designation of the area as a national monument, settlers occupied parts of it and trapped mink, martin and beaver; others cut timber as independent loggers, using hand-logging techniques. These early settlers built small cabins which have since decayed and are now blended into the landscape by new growth. The forests of Misty Fjords are primarily western hemlock and Sitka spruce with lesser amounts of western red cedar and Alaska cedar. There are no stores, services, or phones within the monument. No land within the monument is available for sale. The fjords are bordered by mountains with steep walls, carved by past massive glacial activity. The geology of the area, with its deep valleys and steep slopes, will occasionally nullify radio contact. When cruising the inside fjords like Rudyard Bay, one is out of range to receive or transmit radio calls from marine radio except for boats within view. For some this is disconcerting, but wilderness travel in Alaska provides for a high degree of remoteness and isolation from sights and sounds of other human beings. It does require a high degree of independence and the assumption of risk.

A major boating attraction within the monument is simply to travel slowly and view the scenery. One interesting feature is New Eddystone Rock, a 234-foot-high volcanic plug that stands out of the center of Behm Canal about 22 miles north of its entrance. The Misty Fjord area was volcanic and New Eddystone Rock is a dramatic reminder. Just north of New Eddystone Rock is the entrance to the very scenic Rudyard Bay, with its steep walls and numerous

Punchbowl Lake in Misty Fjords National Monument.

waterfalls. Punchbowl Lake can be reached by a very steep trail that begins at the end of Punchbowl Cove within Rudyard Bay. The Punchbowl Lake trail is considered to be the most scenic within Misty Fjord National Monument. From the lake, steep walls rise several thousand feet almost directly vertically. Trees grow on the wall, and when they reach too great a size and weight, they often fall more than a thousand feet to the lake below. What a splash that must make! Many lakes in the Misty Fjord National Monument have excellent fishing, and good saltwater fishing is also found within Behm Canal. The Misty Fjord streams coming from the mainland section are among the most productive in S.E. Alaska for King salmon.

Cabins, Shelters, and Mooring Buoys

A wilderness area is a piece of land set aside to perpetuate the natural ecosystem, where man is a visitor but does not remain. Alaska is the only state in which man-made structures, such as cabins and shelters (publicly owned), are permitted in a wilderness-designated area. The Alaska National Interest Lands Conservation Act made allowances for public-use cabins in wilderness areas of Alaska because of unique conditions—weather, terrain and remoteness.

The forest service maintains 14 cabins within Misty Fjords National Monument and four Adirondack-type shelters (one side open). My wife and I have stayed at the one at Alava Bay, which is one of two situated on salt water. The other 12 are on freshwater lakes. The cabins have logbooks inside and it is interesting to read about the adventures of other visitors. About ten days before we arrived at the cabin at Alava Bay, there had been a pretty good storm in S.E. Alaska. People before us at the cabin had paddled sea kayaks from the Rudyard Bay area to the cabin and were caught in that squall. Sea kayaks are pretty stable, but it was clear from their notes that their trip had presented a major challenge.

The Inside Passage:
The Canadian and S.E. Alaskan portions - a perspective

From its beginning as a province, British Columbia was incorporated into the mainstream of economic life in Canada, as is witnessed by the extraordinary construction of rail lines across Canada and the development of major ports in both Vancouver and Prince Rupert. The economic development in Alaska (including S.E. Alaska) occurred later than in B.C., and its population growth was much slower. In 1950, the population of S.E. Alaska was 28,000, and by the mid-1990s about 75,000. In contrast, the population of the metropolitan area of Vancouver, B.C., by the mid-1990s reached two million. The logging industry in B.C. was extensively developed at the turn of the century, i.e., the 1900s—long before the logging industry established a foothold in Alaska.

Once the fabled gold rush of the 1890s died off, Alaska was seen as too remote and too wild to develop. Later, several events brought about changes as to how Americans viewed Alaska as a territory and possible exploitation of its natural resources.

The Japanese attacked Alaska in 1942, and while the attack was diversionary, that fact was not immediately clear. The Japanese attack was the singular event that prompted the U.S. government to order the construction of the Alcan Highway. To the credit of engineers, construction crews and the strong cooperation that existed between Canada and the U.S., the Alcan Highway was completed in 1942, just months after the Japanese attack. With a military presence in Alaska, U.S. government officials felt it was important to have some civilian communities in Alaska with stable employment.

The end of the war brought on an even stronger surge in the economic development of Alaska. By the time Japan surrendered, 65 of its cities were devastated, as well as its rail lines and bridges. Japan did not have the timber resources to rebuild, but the U.S. agreed to help Japan reconstruct itself by opening up for the first time on a large scale the vast timber resources of the Tongass National Forest.

In the 1950s, the U.S. Forest Service issued long-term (50-year) timber contracts to two large corporations. One went to a Japanese company, Alaska Pulp Company, who proceeded to build a very large pulp mill in Sitka and a large lumber mill in Wrangell. The second contract went to the Louisiana Pacific Company, who built a large pulp mill in Ketchikan. These two companies for a number of decades provided the largest year-round employment in Alaska. Both are now shut down.

Alaska was granted statehood in 1959, and soon afterwards oil was discovered with vast deposits known to be within the North Slope. The fact that Alaska became a state called for a clarification of who was to control the vast lands of Alaska. Furthermore, before oil reserves could be exploited, land claims by Natives in Alaska had to be resolved.

In addition, conservationists had developed enough public support by the 1960s that their demands for great portions of Alaska be set aside as wilderness had to be considered. The two latter points, i.e., land claims by Alaskan Natives and conservationist demands for preservation of vast tracts of land, were not even on the radar screen when mining and timber harvesting were underway on a huge scale by the late 1800s in California, Oregon, and Washington in the U.S. and in British Columbia, Canada.

The Alaska Native Claims Settlement Act of 1971 (ANCSA)

Several years of negotiations between representatives of the state of Alaska, Alaskan Natives and the federal government resulted in the Alaska Native Claims Settlement Act of 1971. From this Act, Alaskan Natives received 44 million acres of land and $962 million in compensation for the settlement of Aboriginal claims. The state of Alaska was permitted to select its land entitlement under the Statehood Act and to collect, in future years, billions of dollars in royalties, rents and taxes from the development of the North Slope oil fields. The oil companies obtained the rights to develop the North Slope oil fields and to build the oil pipeline from the oil fields to the seaport at Valdez. In addition, millions of acres were set aside for public use. A number of issues remained unresolved, including controversial aspects of the subsistence lifestyle of Alaskan Natives, and the press for stronger protection of lands in Alaska that remained pristine.

The Alaska National Interest Lands Conservation Act

The major conservation groups, both in Alaska and throughout the rest of the United States, campaigned to enact by law the protection of vast lands in Alaska. During Stewart Udall's tenure as Secretary of the Interior, from 1961 to 1969, he laid the groundwork for a national consciousness of protecting wilderness settings by helping establish national trails and the wild-and-scenic river system. His brother, Morris Udall, senator from Arizona and chairman of the powerful Interior Committee, helped push through the Alaska Lands Act. Finally, President Carter convinced Congress to pass the Alaska National Interest Lands Conservation Act of 1980. This protected 104 million acres in Alaska, the single largest conservation action in U.S. history. If Alaska would have been developed and populated within the same time frame as British Columbia, Washington, Oregon and California, these environmental safeguards would not have been considered.

The Talk of Southeast Alaska:
The Tongass National Forest Management Plan

The Tongass National Forest is not simply a park outside of a city like Juneau or Ketchikan. It would be more correct to say that the Tongass National Forest *is* S.E. Alaska. In 1907, Teddy Roosevelt decreed the forests of S.E. Alaska to be the Tongass National Forest. It extends from the Dixon Entrance at the south, on the border with British Columbia, to Yakutat in the north, a distance of about 500 miles; between east and west it is about 120 miles at the widest point. The forest contains more than 1000 islands and more than 11,000 miles of shoreland. Southeast Alaska also includes Glacier Bay National Park, and these two magnificent public lands incorporate about 95 percent of all the land in S.E. Alaska. The remaining 5 percent of the land is where the people live: in Juneau, Ketchikan, Petersburg, Wrangell, Sitka, Haines, Skagway, Hoonah and in dozens of small communities, some with a population of two people. Within that 5 percent of S.E. Alaska is also land given to Natives under the 1971 Alaskan Native Claims Settlement Act.

Multiple use is the management policy that dictates how Tongass National Forest is used. Some uses conflict with other uses. An acre that is preserved for its scenic beauty cannot be logged. Acres that are logged cannot provide a habitat for animals that require old-growth forests. The policy has been controversial. The great percentage of the Tongass National Forest is off-limits to timber harvest, either because the land is designated as wilderness or has a land-use designation as "no harvest" because of its value to tourism. In all, 12.7 million acres within the forest are off-limits to timber harvest. Where permitted, the timber harvest is subject to strict guidelines. These guidelines, under the 1997 Tongass Management Plan, provide a buffer of at least 100 feet from any stream and prevent timber harvest on steep slopes where erosion and landslides may occur. All trees that have an eagle nest, as well as all trees within 330 feet of trees with an eagle nest, are off-limits to cutting. Such guidelines increase the cost of timber harvest in S.E. Alaska and impact employment in the timber industry.

The reasons for the conflict are clear: Conservationists want even less land available for timber harvest, and those with business interests that depend on logging want more. The controversy has stirred public interest in Alaska. When the U.S. Department of Agriculture informed citizens in Alaska about the issues concerning management of the Tongass National Forest and sought comments on draft proposals, they received more than 20,000 responses. That level of public interest is remarkable; however, it is important to remember that the Tongass National Forest is not an Alaskan state forest. It is a national forest and more of us should be informed and interested about policy concerning its management.

The Continuing Legacy of Naturalist John Muir:
Alaskan Forest Reserves

Current and future controversies about the management of U.S. forests can best be understood by considering the important contribution of naturalist John Muir and his influence on President Teddy Roosevelt, as well as the three presidents that preceded Teddy Roosevelt.

When Teddy Roosevelt assumed the presidency of the U.S. in 1901, the total U.S. National Forest Land was just over 46 million acres. Those forest preserves were set aside during the presidential terms of Benjamin Harrison, Grover Cleveland and William McKinley. When Teddy Roosevelt left office in 1909, he had set aside an additional 148 million acres; of that, 17 million acres belong to the Tongass National Forest in S.E. Alaska.

Teddy Roosevelt was well aware of the contribution of John Muir over a period of several decades prior to his administration in arousing public opinion about the values of preserving wilderness. In 1903 Teddy Roosevelt contacted John Muir and expressed the wish that Muir accompany him for a camping and hiking trip into Yosemite so that Muir could point out and explain his concerns about Yosemite and the status of American forests. In May of 1903, the two spent four days alone, hiking through the wilderness of Yosemite. Those four days left a deep impression on Teddy Roosevelt and likely contributed to Roosevelt taking very strong initiatives in setting aside vast amounts of forest as national forests. After the visit with John Muir, he created by presidential proclamation 16 national monuments. The creation of national monuments by presidential proclamation was made possible when Congress passed the Monuments and Antiquities Act. This important congressional action was also made during Roosevelt's administration.

John Muir had earned a well-established national and international reputation as a scientist and naturalist well before his work with Teddy Roosevelt. In 1868 he began exploring the Sierra Nevada range of California, and it was during this time of careful observation and interpretation of mountain landscape that he determined that past glacial activity played a powerful part in modifying the mountain ranges and valleys in the Sierra Nevadas. In 1874 he published his theories of the impact of past glacial activities in his book, *Studies in the Sierra*. Prior to this time, geologists were convinced that the mountain ranges were formed by uplifting, i.e., major tectonic faulting. While uplifting played an important role in the formation of the Sierra Nevada mountain range, the geologists of the time had not considered the significant role played by glaciers. The ideas of John Muir were accepted and made him internationally famous. His interest in glaciers led him to Alaska.

In 1879 John Muir traveled by steamship up the Inside Passage through B.C. waters, crossed the Dixon Entrance, and stopped at Wrangell, Alaska. There he met a missionary, S. Hall Young, who was also interested in exploration. Accompanied by four expert Tlingit Indian canoeists who served as guides, Muir and Hall traveled from Wrangell, through the Wrangell Narrows, to what is now Petersburg. Paddling past Cape Fanshaw in Frederick Sound, they entered Holkham Bay and explored Endicott Arm and Tracy Arm. From there they proceeded north and entered Taku Harbor, then continued around Admiralty Island, stopping at the Native village of Hoonah. His Tlingit guides told Muir of a large bay filled with ice that was retreating. They then paddled to Glacier Bay and explored glaciers, including what is now Muir Glacier, and flora. They then proceeded south, leaving Glacier Bay and returning to Wrangell. This extensive canoe trip of over 700 miles was accomplished in five months. Muir and Hall were perhaps the first Euro-Americans to travel extensively in S.E. Alaska with Tlingit Indians as guides and companions, and in a Native dugout canoe. Muir was the first Euro-American to explore Glacier Bay, when exploration was made possible after significant retreat of the glaciers. He returned to Alaska for more study of glaciers, forests, flora, and wildlife in 1880 and 1890.

This is an example of the small end of the range for private boats.

His extensive travels, combined with his writings and speeches which drew large audiences, made John Muir a powerful and effective spokesman for the importance of wilderness, wildlife and preservation of habitat. He was convinced that the development of a national policy for wildlife preserves, backed by the government was essential to the preservation of wilderness.

Muir's earlier work, prior to his consultations and travel with Teddy Roosevelt, led directly to the following accomplishments of national significance:

Yosemite National Park

In 1889 John Muir and Robert Underwood Johnson, the editor of the *Century*, camped and hiked in Yosemite. While John Muir had extensively traveled and explored this area before, this trip was important because the two discussed the idea of Yosemite being given the status of a national park, thus preventing it from further degradation. One year later the Yosemite National Park Bill passed through Congress, and Yosemite became America's second national park.

United States National Forests

In 1891 Congress passed an act empowering the president to create forest reserves. This had long been proposed by John Muir and led to the establishment of what we now call U.S. national forests. While this act was important, it was still incomplete because it did not establish guidelines for a national policy regarding use of U.S. forests.

The Formation of the Sierra Club

John Muir cofounded the Sierra Club in 1892 and served as president for 22 years. His writings continue to influence this important conservation group. The primary purpose or mission of the Sierra Club is simple and clear: "...to enlist the support and cooperation of the people and the government in preserving the forests and other features of the Sierra Nevada mountains."

Forest Management Plans

In 1896 Congress authorized the establishment of a commission to investigate and form guidelines and policy for the forested lands of the United States. The establishment of national policy to manage our forests had long been argued by John Muir, and the impact of the congressional authorization of 1896 remains in clear evidence today. For example, the six-volume Tongass Land Management Plan Revision (1997) is a current expression of the action taken by the U.S. Congress one hundred years earlier.

Cruising North from Ketchikan: Meyers Chuck

Thirty-eight miles north of Ketchikan, along Clarence Strait is the small community of Meyers Chuck. Meyers Chuck is an excellent natural harbor and has an outstandingly good public dock available for overnight stay at no charge. If the weather gets bad, this is a great retreat. This small community has a population of 35, a good place to experience what life is like in remote, isolated S.E. Alaska. There is an attractive schoolhouse in Meyers Chuck that is now abandoned. The state of Alaska has a policy that public schools will be maintained and operated in rural areas that have eight children or more of school age. In 1997 the community of Meyers Chuck had only three children of school age. Two families with school-aged children moved to Sitka for the academic year; the other family provided home schooling. There is no grocery store or fuel station in Meyers Chuck. In recent years two young brothers have operated a restaurant called the Spruce Needle. The restaurant is in a six-foot-square tree house. It serves two people at a time and a full meal costs $1.50. Karl Wetzel and I ate there in 1996 and enjoyed it very much. The scenery from the tree house restaurant is very much like the scenery in all of the coastal range of S.E. Alaska—wet and green. The two boys who ran the outfit, Noah and Sam, said that they are glad they live in Meyers Chuck because if they lived in a "big city" like Juneau they couldn't operate a restaurant without being hassled by inspectors and all kinds of regulations.

The community, not counting the restaurant, earns its living by commercial fishing and retirement earnings; residents are serious about arts and crafts and have a community art store. They are concerned about Alaska and during the last hearings about the Tongass Management Forest Plan, more than two out of three residents in this small community submitted written comments.

Wrangell

Wrangell is about 90 miles north of Ketchikan, situated at the northern end of Wrangell Island. I normally approach Wrangell from the south, via Ketchikan or Meyers Chuck, by following Clarence and Stikine Strait, then passing north of Woronkoski Island to Wrangell. If I choose to stop at the Anan Bear Observatory on the way to Wrangell, I head east after passing Meyers Chuck and proceed up Ernest Sound past Deer Island to Anan Bay and the observatory. After a visit I proceed to the town of Wrangell by going north along the Eastern Passage on the east side of Wrangell Island. The west side of Wrangell Island, through Zimovia Strait, is also an option.

Wrangell is an interesting, small S. E. Alaskan community with a population of about 2,500 and the distinction of being the only community in the United States that has had three flags of nationality flown over its domain: Russian, British, and American. It is situated just south of the Stikine River, which passes through a mountain range and drains a significant area of British Columbia. From the mouth of the Stikine River, the U.S. Canadian border is about 38 miles to the east; the next several hundred miles of this great river and its tributaries are in Canada.

Wrangell was an important trading point for the Tlingit Indians because of its access along the river to the interior of British Columbia. There are several opportunities in Wrangell to view historic Native sites, including outstandingly preserved petroglyphs on a beach and totem poles on Shakes Island.

Petroglyphs

The petroglyphs at Wrangell—pictorial carvings in stone—were made in ancient times, perhaps 10,000 years

An example of the many petroglyphs one can find.

126

ago. They are open to view on the beach about a mile north-east of the ferry terminal in Wrangell. The most dominant pictorial carvings are geometric, taking the form of an open circle. The open circle, carved in stone, may represent the renewal of life or the return of seasons. Since the Natives who carved the petroglyphs had no written language, assumptions about the meanings remain conjecture. Similar geometric carvings in stone can be seen as far away as Chaco Canyon in New Mexico. They are intriguing to observe and inspect.

Another fine example.

Chief Shakes Community House

Shakes Island is a park on a small island within the Wrangell boat harbor. The park has several totem poles as well as Chief Shakes Community House. In June 1997 I had an opportunity to speak with Nellie Torgemson, who is a granddaughter of Chief Shakes. With her was Nora Rhinehart, an historian of Native culture in Alaska who gives educational talks to tourists on cruise boats that stop in

Wrangell. I asked Nellie Torgemson about her grandfather and his role as chief of the Tlingit Indians in Wrangell.

She explained that she had little recollection of Chief Shakes, but her account of her early childhood was interesting and set the stage for understanding the ever-present fear among Natives in Alaska—and elsewhere—that each generation of Natives, from the time of contact, loses touch with Native history and culture. Nellie Torgemson said she was born in 1932; after her mother died in 1938, she was sent to a boarding school in Haines for Alaskan Natives run by Presbyterian missionaries. At the school "...we learned nothing about Indians—nothing!" She went on to say "...the Presbyterians made it a rule that elders couldn't teach Native language, culture or the old ways. Up the road from our boarding house in Haines there was an Indian village, and once we were invited to a potlatch, but we couldn't go because a potlatch ceremony was thought to be pagan. There were about 50 Native children at the Haines House. Native children were not used to experiencing physical punishment because it is not how Natives discipline their children. But at the Haines House, we were physically punished, and I remember being beaten with a stick. Speaking our Native language was one of the things that would bring on punishment. Once and then again, someone would run away. But there were people who earned money—so much a head— to recapture a runaway child and return the child to the boarding school."

She continued, "I believe they [the staff at the boarding school] figured it was best for us to forget about our culture and become like white people. That is why they did not teach us any history of our own people. The world would be a better place if the civilized world would have learned from Natives. Indians knew which roots and herbs had medicinal value, and they knew how to survive. But the attitude was that if the Indians made something, it wasn't any good."

Chief Shakes Longhouse.

Nellie Torgemson expressed puzzlement that Alaska, as we know it, was purchased from the Russians. She said the Russians never set foot into the interior of Alaska: "So, how could they possibly have sold it?"

The comments made by Nellie Torgemson about her childhood and her lack of personal contact with her grandfather and other elders who could have taught her Native language, history, culture and traditions go beyond an isolated experience; they reflect deeply ingrained public policy. Significant government policies that shaped the lives of Natives after the time of contact are on exhibit at the Museum at Warm Springs, in Central Oregon.

The Museum at Warm Springs has many displays of traditional Native artwork as well as information about the meaning of the Columbia River salmon in the lives of Indians who lived along the Columbia River east of the

Cascade Mountains. The museum wanted to portray some past government practices that were destructive to the Indians in Central Oregon. They did so by displaying within the museum direct quotes from the Bureau of Indian Affairs from the late 1800s. Below are two quotes, one dealing with language suppression and the other urging that Native children be removed from their parents.

Regarding Native language training versus English language training:

The instruction of Indians in the vernacular is not only of no use to them, but is detrimental to the cause of their education and civilization, and no school will be permitted on the reservation in which the English language is not exclusively taught.

Commissioner of Indian Affairs　February 2, 1887

Regarding the raising of Indian children:

The children should be boarded by the schoolteacher and entirely taken from their parents or guardians, for without that the school is of little benefit to the children.

Myron Reaves　　1863

The silence of Christians about how they converted Native Americans.

The Protestant effort to convert Native Americans to Christianity required that they give up their cultural identity, their language and their children. By these sacrifices on the part of their parents, the Native children were to become civilized and have their souls saved. I thought to myself, surely there must have been Christian religious leaders during the 1800s and early 1900s who questioned this missionary policy and spoke against it. In fact, no religious leader in the U.S. spoke against this policy of cultural destruction. I uncovered the writings of Herman Melville and Carl Jung who were opposed to the destructive impact of missionary zeal on Natives. What they wrote and the reactions they received from their writings explains decades of silence on the missionary impact on Natives.

In his youth Herman Melville spent three years on whaling ships and became an expert on these ships, various species of whales and their characteristics, and intricate details of actual hunts and killings of whales. While in the South Pacific, he also observed firsthand, during a four-month stay in the Polynesian Islands, the destructive effects of European conquest and missionary conversion on the life of Native Polynesians. What he witnessed was the taking of traditional Native lands for huge profits by colonists without regard for the human rights of the Natives. He also witnessed that the missionaries kept a blind eye to the economic exploitation that beset the Natives and disregarded even the possibility that the Natives' traditional religious beliefs had any spiritual significance.

Melville wrote the novel *Typee*, which glamorized the allure of Polynesian women against a background of scenic beauty, sea travel and adventure. The original draft included about 30 pages of text that exposed political and economic exploitation of Polynesians and the negative impact of missionary evangelism on Polynesians. John Wiley, the publisher, was shocked by the antimissionary and political exposé of the novel and insisted that the 30 pages be deleted. The novel was published in 1846, minus the 30 pages.

A Second Look at *Moby Dick*

Most authors neither forgive nor forget when they believe that an important piece of their work has been arbitrarily rejected, and Melville was no exception. In fact, he wrote to his friend Hawthorne in 1851 and complained, "What I feel most moved to write, that is banned—it will not pay. Yet, altogether, write the other way I cannot."

I reread the great epic novel *Moby Dick* with the knowledge that Melville's first effort to portray profound abuse of indigenous peoples was rejected. I believe that Melville rewrote those 30 rejected pages and threaded them throughout *Moby Dick*. Consider the following points:

1. Pequod, the whaling ship in *Moby Dick*, was named after an Indian Tribe in Massachusetts that had ceased to exist.
2. The three harpoonists on the Pequod were indigenous men; Queesqueg, a Polynesian; Tashtego, a Native Indian from the area of Martha's Vineyard; and Daggoo, a black African.
3. The white whale (Moby Dick) is described by symbolism of all powerful and privileged Western Christian civilization. In the chapter entitled "The Whiteness of the Whale," we see both the author's struggle to convey the power and the fearsomeness of the white whale as well as the beauty, the spirituality and the dread the symbolism is meant to convey. "It was the whiteness of the whale that above all things appalled me. But how can I hope to explain myself here; and yet, in some dim, random way, explain myself I must, else all these chapters might be naught."

4. White, as a color, has powerful religious significance. "...in the higher mysteries of the most august religions it has been made the symbol of the divine spotlessness and power." And, "...white is specially employed in the celebration of the Passion of our Lord; though in the Vision of St. John, white robes are given to the redeemed, and the four-and-twenty elders stand clothed in white before the great white throne, and the Holy One that sitteth there white like wool; yet for all these accumulated associations, with whatever is sweet, and honorable, and sublime, there yet lurks an elusive something in the innermost idea of his hue, which strikes more of panic to the soul than the redness which affrights in blood."

5. Melville's description of the white whale also includes symbolism that the white race has power over others. "...this preeminence in it applies to the human race itself, giving the white man ideal mastership over every dusky tribe."

Melville also incorporates in *Moby Dick* a significant reference to the Biblical account of Jonah who tried to escape the task of giving a message from God to sinners by sailing away on a ship. God created a monster storm and Jonah, recognizing that his sin caused God to create a great storm, leaped from the ship to spare the other crew. His sin was failing to give a message. Like Jonah, Melville failed in his effort to give a direct message. In *Moby Dick* we have his message in the form of an allegory.

The writings of Carl Jung vis-à-vis missionary evangelism of Indians.

Carl Jung was born in Switzerland in 1875. He earned an M.D. degree and specialized in psychiatry. He was influenced by Sigmund Freud, but developed his own theories. He was particularly interested in studying the potential enriching effects of religion and spirituality in human development throughout the lifespan. He traveled extensively and spent much time with indigenous peoples to learn of their religious beliefs. He openly declared himself to be Christian; however, he was deeply concerned with and opposed to the tactics of Christian missionaries who discredited the religious beliefs of Indians and attempted to eradicate their religious beliefs.

In the early 1900s he spent several months in New Mexico and befriended Ochwiay Biano (Mountain Lake) who was chief of the Taos Pueblos. He quotes Mountain Lake: "Why do the Americans not let us alone? Why do they want to forbid our dances? Why do they make difficulties when we want to take our young people from school in order to lead them to the Kiva (site of the rituals) and instruct them in our religion? We do nothing to harm the Americans! The Americans want to stamp out our religion. Why can they not let us alone?"

Though deeply religious himself, the writings of Carl Jung were not well received by dogma-oriented Christian leaders. A number of times he stated, "They would have burned me as a heretic in the Middle Ages!"

His reference to being burned as a heretic may have been prompted by his memory of the fate of Michael Servetus (1511-1553). Servetus published a book about a Unitarian view of God as opposed to the dogma of the Trinity. John Calvin was outraged and brought charges against Servetus. He was found guilty of heresy and burned at the stake.

The effort to suppress indigenous religious beliefs continues to this day and appears in many forms. In 1954 the

Church of Jesus Christ of Latter-day Saints formalized a missionary program known as the Indian Student Placement Program. The program is voluntary in that Indian natural parents sign a release form to permit their children to participate. This is in contrast to previous and more egregious times when federal law permitted children to be removed from Native natural parents and compelled to attend missionary schools, even without the consent of the parents. The stated purpose of the program is to train the Native children in Mormon beliefs and lifestyle. Indian parents are discouraged from visiting the children, especially during the first year. George Patrick Lee, who was a member of the Church of Jesus Christ of Latter-day Saints, spoke against the Indian Student Placement Program. He expressed concern that the program would suppress Native Indian culture. Mr. Lee was excommunicated in 1988.

The Times They Are A-Changing

I believe that attitudes towards Natives in Alaska have changed and, compared with a hundred years ago, most people respect their endurance, their art and their culture. I have spoken with preachers in Alaska who speak with regret about the repression that was practiced for many years by missionaries who believed that removing all traces of a "pagan" culture was in the best interest of Native peoples in Alaska. The effort to assimilate Native children included removing children from their families, forbidding them to speak their Native language, and preventing them from practicing Native religious beliefs. However, the roots of prejudice run deep and the effects of oppression last for generations. In 1978 Congress finally enacted the American Indian Religious Freedom Act. This was 132 years after the publication of the novel by Herman Melville, whose message about religious persecution of Indians was suppressed.

Other things are changing in Alaska as well, especially those industries which had been mainstays of the economy in S.E. Alaska—timber and fishing.

APC Sawmill closes in Wrangell

On November 30, 1994, the Japanese-owned APC Sawmill closed. It had been the largest employer in Wrangell (225 direct employees, plus support contractors) and had contributed 30 percent of Wrangell's payroll wages. As I walked through the company grounds and spoke with the sole caretaker, I was reminded of visiting Namu in British Columbia. One difference was that Namu was a company town, and when the cannery closed all jobs ceased (except for one caretaker) and the town was vacated. Wrangell has other sources of employment, including commercial fishing and tourism, but the impact of the plant closure was serious and continues to affect the economy in retail, wholesale, and service sectors.

This sawmill, the largest employer in Wrangell, closed in 1994.

The sawmill closed because the company believed that it did not have a guarantee of timber supply that it could harvest in sufficient quantities to earn a profit. Changes in the Tongass Land Management Plan, which is more restrictive than in the past, contributed to the company decision. I spoke with a number of residents of Wrangell, and many expressed the view that restriction of timber harvest was warranted even though the economic effects are serious. Some have found other ways to make a living. For example, one man said that, after he lost his mill job, he applied for a license to be a fishing and hunting guide and now earns a living using the skills that he had developed earlier as a hobby. With great satisfaction, he showed me a collection of photographs of outdoor adventures he has guided since the mill closure. But without doubt, a significant number of families in Wrangell are struggling financially as a direct result of the mill closure. (More on changes in the commercial fishing industry follow in the section on Petersburg.)

The Anan Creek Bear Observatory

About 30 miles south of Wrangell is Anan Creek, which has a phenomenal annual run of pink salmon. To get to the Anan Creek Bear Observatory from Wrangell, come around the northern tip of Wrangell Island and proceed south along the Eastern Passage. Anan Bay is south of Wrangell Island and on the mainland, at the juncture of Ernest Sound and Bradford Canal. The area can only be reached by boat or float plane. A small bay provides good anchorage; a dinghy is needed to get to shore. There are no docks. From shore a trail of about one and a half miles follows the creek to a platform, which is the main part of the bear observatory.

The salmon run starts around mid-July, and for about seven weeks the river is almost clogged with hundreds of thousands of returning salmon. Both black bears and brown bears come to feast on these salmon, as well as many bald eagles.

Salmon runs are huge in many of the streams in Southeast Alaska.

Upon arrival visitors are met by a forest service employee who provides a "trail talk" about bears and how to behave in bear territory. One of his points is the importance of staying on the trail or on the observation platform—and having no food on their person. Thanks to those simple rules, the

Leif & Marge Terdal at the Anan Creek Bear Observatory.

bears have become habituated to human presence in the area and, while aware, they ignore visitors. When my wife and I visited the area, the ranger told us that there have been no examples of bears in the area getting food from people. From the platform, we watched and photographed four black bears for several hours. We also saw a large

Brown bears feeding on the plentiful pink salmon.

brown bear sow with three cubs. We were sometimes within 40 feet of the bears, but they ignored us and were quite occupied with catching salmon. They were remarkably agile, as they walked through the fast current of the river and caught salmon either with their paws or with their mouth. We saw one large black bear catch and eat seven salmon in one hour; the forest ranger at the platform said she saw the same bear catch and eat 20 salmon in one two-and-a-half-hour feed. The bears have somewhat different individual styles. Some "snorkel" or put their head in the river and catch the salmon with their jaws; others use their paws. Age and experience counts a lot. We saw experienced bears catch salmon consistently in about 30 seconds after positioning themselves over a choice spot. Two-year-old cubs—though large—would take 20 minutes to catch a salmon. From my observations—confirmed by several forest rangers—mother bears are excellent teachers and stay with their cubs for about two and a half years or until the cubs can fish and gather other foods successfully.

Rangers at the Anan Creek Bear Observatory have told me that they average about 2500 visitors a season, for an average of 50 persons a day. The ranger felt that number

Another brown bear catches a tasty snack.

was manageable, but that with larger numbers, the bears would possibly become uncomfortable and leave the area. The Forest Service is considering the option of requiring a permit to limit the number of people at Anan Creek to a manageable number. At present, the number of visitors is limited somewhat in that the number of guides who are permitted to take clients to Anan Creek Bear Observatory is restricted, and each guide has a fixed number of client slots per season that cannot be exceeded. So far there is not a limitation on coming to the bear observatory via a private boat. Obviously, cruise ships are not allowed.

Petersburg

Petersburg is about 40 miles from Wrangell. To get there from Wrangell, proceed west about 20 miles and arrive at

Point Alexander on Mitkof Island, in Sumner Strait. This places you at the entrance to Wrangell Narrows which consists of 21 miles of a fairly narrow waterway, but it is well marked with 66 navigational markers. Even so, I would not recommend passage during a fog.

Tidal currents are strong in Wrangell Narrows. To use the current to your advantage, enter the Narrows on the last part of the flood tide. Plan to arrive halfway through the Narrows at slack high tide; then the current will be with you again as you continue on to Petersburg. Along the banks of this beautiful passage are many recreational cabins, not a common sight in S.E. Alaska. There is excellent Chinook salmon fishing within the narrows, with the peak of the salmon run in May and June. Bald eagles are very numerous and it is not uncommon to see 40 or more of these magnificent birds at a time.

Petersburg was founded by Peter Buschman, who arrived in the area in 1897 from Norway and found that the location had a suitable area for a harbor and excellent fishing for halibut and salmon. What added to his interest was the large amounts of ice from the Le Conte Tidewater Glacier that flows to the area. He recognized that fishermen could ship the abundant halibut and salmon from the area to ports south, such as Seattle, chilled on ice, rather than canned or salted. Fresh fish brought a substantially better price. He encouraged his friends from Norway to come to the area and build a town. The town continues to have a very productive fishery for salmon, halibut, and shrimp. During the summer fishing season, the cold storage plants and the canneries work 24 hours a day. From the attractive harbor, the noise from the fishing operations can be heard throughout the night.

Petersburg remains a prosperous and very busy small town; however, fishermen at the dock speak with considerable concern about changes in the salmon industry. The problem is not a shortage of salmon (at least not in Alaska), but of such huge numbers of salmon on the world market that the prices are less than half (adjusted for inflation) of what they were ten and 15 years ago. Vast numbers of pen-reared salmon, mostly from Norway and Chile, glut the world market. It is now almost impossible for someone to enter the business of commercial salmon fishing as a new entry, purchase a boat, gear, and license, and earn a living. The two resource-based industries in Alaska, fishing and timber harvest, are undergoing serious challenges and changes.

Alaska's Commercial Fishing Industry: Diverse and Strong

The salmon component of the commercial fishing industry in Alaska is in dire trouble because of the severe drop in prices paid to fishermen for ocean-caught salmon. However, Alaskan fishermen catch many more kinds of fish, including halibut, pollock, sablefish, cod rockfish, and others. Alaskan waters also produce prodigious amounts of crab, shrimp, scallops, clams, and other seafood. Alaskan fishermen harvest more seafood than fishermen in all the other 49 states combined. More than 70,000 Alaskans earn their living at sea.

The Sons of Norway Lodge

The Sons of Norway lodge in Petersburg features a buffet dinner several times a week with salmon, halibut, shrimp, crab, salads, rice, potatoes, and ample Norwegian pastries and other desserts. Following dinner some local people put on a program of Norwegian dances and music. It is great fun. If you are in Petersburg, check with the harbor master about location and schedules for the Sons of Norway dinners. This buffet dinner experience is but one example of the continuing presence of Norwegian traditions in Petersburg. On May 17 each year, there is a major ceremony commemorating the anniversary of the Norwegian Constitution.

Frederick Sound and Stephens Passage: Petersburg to Juneau

The distance between Petersburg and Juneau is only 108 miles; however, the scenic wonders along the way are so outstanding that rushing through to get from one place to the other is not recommended. A mountain range starting from the Stikine River (25 miles below Petersburg) continues north about 100 miles, many of its peaks exceeding 10,000 feet, and marks the border between Alaska and British Columbia. This range has enormous ice fields and active glaciers, which come into view when one leaves Petersburg and enters Frederick Sound. The Le Conte Glacier (about 20 miles south of Petersburg) is the southernmost tidewater glacier in North America and releases very large amounts of ice. Just north of Petersburg is Thomas Bay with Baird Glacier providing very scenic views—although the glacier has retreated and is no longer a tidewater glacier. Further to the north in Holkham Bay is the famous Tracy Arm with Sawyer Glacier; also in the same area (to the south) is Endicott Arm and Dawes Glacier. All of these glaciers draw from a continuous mass of snow pack on a mountain range extending about 100 miles.

About 35 miles north of Petersburg in Frederick Sound is Cape Fanshaw, a prominent cape that marks the point where Stephens Passage begins and opens into a wide sea passage to the north. Frederick Sound continues to the west of Cape Fanshaw and connects with Chatham Strait.

A humpback whale passes by.

Frederick Sound is a major passageway for salmon and halibut and also for humpback whales. While humpback whales may be seen in northern British Columbia waters, they are seen more frequently in Alaskan waters, especially north of Frederick Sound and on up to Glacier Bay, Icy

Frederick Sound outside of Petersburg.

144

Strait, Lynn Canal and also on both sides of Admiralty Island. After spending their summers feeding in the cold and food-rich Alaskan waters, they swim back to the waters off Hawaii for the winter months, with calves born in late winter.

A wonderful sight.

Because the waters just north and west of Cape Fanshaw are quite open, the sea conditions can become rough should the weather turn windy, especially if combined with strong tidal currents. A place to keep in mind for shelter is on the southeast side of Whitney Island, just a few miles north of Cape Fanshaw.

Hobart Bay

Another option if shelter is needed is the excellent moorage available on Entrance Island in Hobart Bay, about 17 miles north of Cape Fanshaw. Entrance Island has a public float maintained by the state. Should the weather be difficult at all, you will likely meet some other boaters seeking protection in this cove. There is a private residence on Entrance Island where a family with two daughters lives. Both parents are commercial crabbers and also fish for halibut. They home-school their children, and the nearest community is Petersburg where they go by boat to sell their crabs and halibut and buy food and supplies. They told me that the state of Alaska provides substantial, ongoing support to parents who must home-school their children because they live in remote areas. This young family of four make up the entire population of Entrance Island, and both adults took the time to write a letter expressing their views when the Tongass Forest Management Plan was undergoing review and revision. From the public dock you can see their house and their two commercial crab boats.

The state float in Hobart Bay on Entrance Island.

Admiralty Island National Monument

In 1978, by presidential proclamation, the Admiralty Island National Monument was established. As was the case for the other national monument in S.E. Alaska (Misty Fjord National Monument), the Alaska National Interest Lands Conservation Act (ANILCA) designated most of the acreage within the Admiralty Island National Monument as wilderness. The wilderness designation keeps the land off-limits to timber, mining, and other commercial activities. Admiralty Island was established as a monument to recognize and give special protection to its unique ecological, geological, cultural, prehistoric, and scientific values. Congress omitted from designation the Green Creek Mine on Admiralty Island. The mine has the largest known deposits of silver in North America.

Admiralty Island is a very large island, about 100 miles long and 40 miles wide. It is bordered on the west by Chatham Strait, on the south by Frederick Sound, and on the east by Stephens Passage. Mansfield Peninsula, on the northern part of the island, was not included in the national monument.

The monument includes the Kootznahoo Wilderness, "fortress of the bears" in the language of the Tlingit people. Admiralty Island has the largest concentration of brown bears in S.E. Alaska. An important viewing place to observe brown bears is the Pack Creek Bear Observatory, which is located in Seymour Canal, just west of Windfall Island. Permits are required and visitors are limited to 24 a day. The limitation was established by agreement of the Alaska Department of Fish and Game and the U.S. Forest Service and is based on assumptions of how much human presence the bears can tolerate without causing disruption to their lives. Those who have an opportunity to observe these great animals in a natural setting view it as an overwhelmingly positive experience. Visitors on private boats (with a permit) can approach the area of the Pack Creek

Bear Observatory by boating up Seymour Canal from Stephens Passage. Within Seymour Canal is Tiedeman Island which includes exceptional high-density eagle nesting habitat.

The Pack Creek Bear Observatory

In July 1998, my wife and I visited the Pack Creek Bear Observatory as part of a nine-day boating trip in which we planned to see bears, whales and ice. We left Wrangell and traveled on to Petersburg and from there entered Holkham Bay and toured Tracy Arm, marveling at the steep-walled fjord and the north and south Sawyer Glaciers. Although Pack Creek is just west of Holkham Bay, I knew we would run short of fuel. After leaving Tracy Arm, we went north to Juneau, obtained fuel and groceries and went south and spent the night at Taku Harbor. We left early in the morning of July 31 and arrived at the anchorage near the sand spit (mouth of Pack Creek) just before noon. We anchored and rowed our dinghy to shore. We were met by Russel Hood, who works for the Admiralty Island National Monument as a forest service worker and bear expert. After checking our permits he provided an orientation to Pack Creek and gave us information about brown bears and how to behave in their presence. We then walked about a third of a mile to an observation viewpoint which overlooked Pack Creek as it entered a sand spit and tidewater in Seymour Canal. We saw five brown bears, although one departed into the forest soon after we arrived and did not return. We had the opportunity to view the other four for about three hours before they moved out of sight. The bears alternated between some serious and successful salmon fishing and some rough play. As at the Anan Bear Observatory, we saw that the bears seemed to have individual styles in pursuing salmon. Some stayed in one prime spot, placed their head in the water and came up with a salmon in their jaws. Others used their paws. Some stayed at one spot and waited, others ran up the stream with salmon, scurrying to avoid capture.

I asked Russel how it was that the U.S. Forest Service came to understand that brown bears and black bears can be safely viewed in the wild, without great risk to human life. He explained that the U.S. Forest Service did not discover the principle but that local people in Alaska—such as from Wrangell and Petersburg—had a long-standing tradition of entering the wilderness to view bears without hunting them and being impeccably careful about food. Some of these people campaigned for special areas that prohibited hunting. Pack Creek, for example, has been banned from hunting since the 1930s.

After returning to Wrangell at the end of our nine-day boating trip, we recalled that we had seen more than two dozen bears—including those at the two bear observatories, plus a few along beaches—and many humpback whales, especially at Cape Fanshaw. The greatest amount of ice and number of large bergs that we saw were at Le Conte, North America's southernmost tidewater glacier and one that sheds a prodigious amount of ice. In all we had traveled over 600 miles by boat, put 45 hours on our engine and used 179 gallons of diesel fuel.

Below is more information about Tracy Arm and other points along the way between Petersburg and Juneau.

Tracy Arm

About 20 miles north of Hobart Bay and within Stephens Passage is Holkham Bay. This is a very scenic area, and a major attraction is Tracy Arm, a 22-mile-long fjord which leads to both North Sawyer Glacier and South Sawyer Glacier. The area is spectacular with steep-walled granite cliffs

The Second Effort in LeConte Bay.

exceeding a height of 2000 feet. The fjord is exceptionally deep. Beautiful waterfalls dot the passage. The most striking feature is the numerous and large icebergs that calve off these active tidewater glaciers. Wildlife is abundant. The entire Stephens Passage, including the area near Holkham Bay, is a prime viewing area for humpback whales. Within Tracy Arm, seals are commonly observed on floating icebergs, and bald eagles are abundant.

Taku Harbor

About 20 miles north of Holkham Bay is Taku Harbor, which provides good anchorage and a state float. It is an important place of refuge in case of bad weather. Ruins of a large, abandoned cannery lie east of the public floats.

A few miles north of the small Taku Harbor is Taku Inlet, which cuts 15 miles into a mountain range. Norris Glacier and Taku Glacier, as well as snow-capped peaks, can be seen from this Inlet. From the inlet, a range of mountains extends north all the way past Juneau to Skagway. A number of glaciers draw from this huge ice field, including the famous Mendenhall Glacier just north of Juneau.

Juneau

Coming from the south in Stephens Passage, Juneau is about 12 miles north of Point Arden, on Admiralty Island. A point to consider about approaching the Juneau area by boat is whether to head up the Gastineau Channel for a direct route to Juneau or to go around Douglas Island and obtain moorage at Auke Bay. The distance from Point Arden to Auke Bay is about 26 miles. The advantage of Auke Bay as a moorage area is that it places you much closer to points north, such as Skagway, or west, such as Glacier Bay. If you choose to moor your vessel in Juneau, you probably will have to go south and then around Douglas Island before proceeding to either Skagway or to Glacier Bay. The reason is that the northern part

The Mendenhall Glacier near Juneau.

of Gastineau Channel—from Juneau—is very shallow and only passable during high tide. Another advantage of obtaining moorage in Auke Bay, rather than Juneau, is that Auke Bay provides moorage exclusively for transient boaters, whereas the marinas in Juneau lease permanent moorage and spots are only available for transients when a local has temporarily vacated his spot. There is good public transportation from Auke Bay to downtown Juneau and also to Mendenhall Glacier.

Juneau is a major city of interest for travelers plying the Inside Passage. The capital of Alaska, Juneau is a small city with a population of about 30,000—nearly one-half the population of S.E. Alaska. About half of the work force in Juneau is involved with government work, including federal, state, and local government operations. Set against Mount Juneau to the east and Gastineau Channel to the west, Juneau is a beautiful city in a remarkable setting. Historic buildings include the St. Nicholas Russian Orthodox Church built in 1894. The Alaskan State Museum is excellent and provides interesting and educational information about Native cultures in Alaska, the Russian period, the gold strike and gold mining, and wildlife and habitat in Alaska.

Juneau is the headquarters for the SeaAlaska Corporation, a successful Native Alaskan corporation with operations in the timber industry, fishing, and tourism.

Hoonah

Hoonah is located on the northeast shore of Chichagof Island, about 70 miles by boat from Juneau (43 miles from Auke Bay) and only 20 miles across Icy Strait from the entrance to Glacier Bay. To get there from Auke Bay, proceed northwest and go through Saginaw Channel between

Shelter Island and the northern tip of Mansfield Peninsula. Proceed south in Chatham Strait; turn west after passing Couverden Island and head west into Icy Strait. Enter Port Frederick after passing the navigational marker at Inner Point Sophia. The harbor is about one-half mile south of the Alaska State Ferry Terminal. It is an excellent harbor, perhaps the best in S.E. Alaska. Many boaters who are waiting to enter Glacier Bay National Park wait at Hoonah should they arrive earlier than the date their permit allows entrance to the park.

In July 1997, my wife and I met Ichirou Moriwaki, who had just sailed from Osaka, Japan, in his 26-foot sailboat,

In his 26-foot sailboat, this young man traveled from Tokyo, Japan, to Alaska as part of a four-year around-the-world adventure.

the Aurora. Hoonah was his first landfall after leaving Japan, and he arrived safely about ten days before his scheduled entrance to Glacier Bay. He spoke good English and mentioned that he had met two families from Australia, who had crossed the Pacific from the Southern Hemisphere to tour Alaska and visit Glacier Bay National Park. The park is a World Heritage Site and draws visitors who love adventure and who appreciate the level of ecological protection that is maintained by the park management. Ichirou gave me the address of his parents in Japan and asked me to write them. He then said: "I will write you in 2002 when I return from my around-the-world cruise." The small community of Hoonah (population 900) is the largest settlement of Tlingit Indians in S.E. Alaska. The Natives settled there about 250 years ago when the glaciers advanced in Glacier Bay and forced them to move. The economy of Hoonah, like much of S.E. Alaska, is based on natural resources, commercial fishing, primarily salmon and halibut, and the timber industry. As in many other places in Alaska, residents make substantial use of subsistence hunting and fishing to supplement their food supply.

The community of Hoonah suffered a serious fire in 1942 that destroyed many residences and, unfortunately, many historic Tlingit cultural artifacts, including totem poles, ceremonial masks and other art forms. There is a community cultural center that is well worth visiting, but it is not as comprehensive in its display of artifacts as it would have been had the destructive fire not occurred.

Glacier Bay National Park

Glacier Bay National Park is pristine wilderness and the world's largest wildlife preserve. Twelve glaciers reach tidewater within the park, bringing with them huge amounts of ice formed by substantial precipitation falling as snow on very high mountains within the park, including Mount Fairweather at 15,300 feet in elevation. Once within the park a boat operator must radio the office at Bartlett Cove and give the approximate time of arrival at the park headquarters. Checking in at the park headquarters for an orientation is required.

I recommend that you bring with you to the orientation your navigational chart of Glacier Bay. The orientation is highly individualized, since only 25 private boats are permitted in the park at any one time between June 1 and August 31. The park ranger will review the rules of the Park concerning boat speed within the park, how to handle your boat so as not to disturb the whales and other marine mammals, and which areas are off-limits when seals and sea lions have their pups or when birds are nesting. The park ranger will also give information about best places to anchor and to view wildlife. The whole park is excellent for viewing humpback whales, but if you are interested in seeing bears and mountain goats, the park ranger will give you current information. You can record this information in your chart and thus not rely on memory. The quality of the information during the orientation is superb. The park employees are knowledgeable and view Glacier Bay as sacred ground and a World Heritage Site—which it is.

Bartlett Cove contains the park headquarters and an excellent restaurant and lodging facilities. Fuel for boats is available at the dock but nowhere else in the park. Groceries are not available, nor newspapers. Bartlett Cove has trails that permit you to hike in a "new" rain forest, formed since the retreat of the massive ice pack and glaciers in the last 100 years. Once you leave Bartlett Cove by boat to explore the vast park, there will be no trails, no docks and no mooring buoys. You are on your own and your boating skills and ability to be independent and self-reliant will be tested.

My first visit to Glacier Bay National Park was in late June 1996. I planned to meet my wife at the airport in Juneau, where she was to join me on our boat for the trip to Glacier Bay. Unfortunately, a family emergency prevented her from doing so. I left solo on June 22 from Juneau and proceeded south along Gastineau Channel and went on the west side of Douglas Island, then north to Point Retreat on the northern tip of Admiralty Island, then south to enter Icy Strait and on up toward the entrance of the park. The weather was excellent until I passed Port Frederick on the northern part of Chichagof Island. The wind blew hard from the west and the waters began to get rough. I was well into Icy Strait when winds from Cross Sound came blustering in from the west. The winds blew very hard but what scared me the most was seeing a wall of clouds that rose about 7000 feet above the highest hills to the west of me. It was both beautiful and frightening. I knew a storm was coming, and since I was alone I chose not to stop the boat to take a picture. I was afraid to give up valuable time should the weather worsen—which it did. I kept going north toward the entrance to the park. That evening, as I approached Bartlett Cove, I thought about the trip and realized that the last 25 miles of the journey from Juneau took as much time as the first 65 miles. Standing waves and high wind slowed my progress to a crawl. The Bartlett Cove area offers protection during stormy weather, and once I reached the cove, the waters were calm though the wind still howled. After checking in for the orientation and getting information about the park, I spent the night anchored in the waters at Bartlett Cove.

The next morning I headed up into the bay and pulled into Sandy Cove (about 20 miles from Bartlett Cove) and anchored. Sandy Cove provides a very good anchorage and is a good starting point to either head north into Muir Inlet to view some glaciers or west to view Reid Glacier and further in to John Hopkins Inlet or Tarr Inlet. I waited in Sandy Cove for a break in the weather. Rain fell nearly continuously and fog hugged the surrounding hills like a blanket, occasionally lifting to several hundred feet above ground level. I did watch several bears along the beach at Sandy Cove and saw some sea otters. Two other boats were anchored nearby.

The weather did not improve and I was reluctant to proceed in the fog to Reid Inlet; after two days I pulled anchor and headed back into Bartlett Cove and anchored. I rowed my dinghy to shore and checked in again at the park office to check on the weather forecast. More storm fronts were expected with about an eight-hour break between them. That night the wind blew about 40 knots per hour. I woke up several times to check to see that my anchor was holding. The next morning I left early and headed back to Juneau; I saw six humpback whales at Point Adolphus as I was leaving the park which renewed my determination to return some day to this great place and hope for better weather. I made the trip back to Juneau in six hours. Another front came in that night, and on Sunday, June 30, a very strong storm hit S.E. Alaska with 2.25 inches of rain in Juneau and sustained winds of 45 knots gusting to 55 knots. I was safely at harbor in Juneau and waited the weather out. The next day the weather cleared.

Glacier Bay: Second trip on Second Effort

Exactly one year to the day after my first trip to Glacier Bay, I left with my wife, Marge, from Juneau to explore again the wonders of this great park. As we left Juneau on June 22, 1997, we talked about my trip the year earlier and the wet, windy and foggy weather. This reminded us of past outdoor experiences under similar circumstances, such as camping and hiking in wet and windy weather, which was good preparation for exploring S.E. Alaska.

As my wife and I approached Glacier Bay, we saw the huge snow-capped mountain range in front of us. We were in the midst of clear skies and calm waters. From time to time we saw humpback whales surfacing and diving below the surface of the waters with their tale flukes hanging almost motionless in the air. We checked in at Bartlett Cove and headed out for our first-night's anchorage at Berg Bay; we saw two whales outside of Glacier Bay Lodge as we left but saw no other wildlife on our trip to our first anchorage at Berg Bay. We left the next morning early and stopped briefly at Blue Mouse Cove, a protective cove, and headed into the west arm of Glacier Bay. We began to see large ice chunks and larger icebergs. We arrived at Reid Inlet that afternoon and anchored on the west side. We dropped our dinghy, rowed to shore, and hiked along a glacial moraine up close to the face of the glacier. We saw many signs of bear, as well as a fascinating bird—the oyster catcher. This bird has a bright red beak and engages in dramatic antics, apparently to distract potentially harmful folk away from her offspring. We returned by dinghy back to our boat, and as nightfall came, I spent much time in the cockpit at the back of the boat looking for signs of wildlife. A large brown bear appeared that evening and walked along the glacial moraine.

The next morning we left Reid Glacier and very slowly moved through that section of Glacier Bay into Blue Mouse Cove and anchored. We hiked along the shore primarily to stretch our legs and get off our boat. We saw moose droppings and talked to a biology research team studying intertidal areas. As we returned to our boat, we met two biologists who were housed at the small park service houseboat at Blue Mouse Cove. They had been to Reid Glacier the night before—as we had been—and talked about the large brown bear that appeared along the glacial moraine.

Moored by Reid Glacier.

We left Blue Mouse Cove at 1 p.m. and arrived at Sandy Cove east of Puffin Island at 2:30 p.m. Two other boats were moored there. We ate lunch and then paddled our small dinghy to shore. We came upon an area where bears sleep—the indentations in the grasses were about 12 feet by 5 feet. We had no interest in challenging a bear and left shortly after and rowed back to our boat. We watched from the back of our boat and spotted a total of nine bears strolling along the shore.

The next morning we left Sandy Cove. As we approached South Marble Island on our way back to Bartlett Cove, we saw many sea lions, humpback whales, and lots of bird life. We anchored at Bartlett Cove, paddled ashore, hiked, revisited the lodge, and ate dinner at the lodge. Our entire stay at Glacier Bay on this trip was graced with sunny and warm weather—unusual, but we enjoyed it. As we left the next day to return to Juneau, we reflected on our visit to this remarkable place—Glacier Bay National Park. S.E. Alaska has many wonders. What is special about Glacier Bay National Park is not just the mountains, fjords, glaciers, whales, and wildlife but the knowledge that Glacier Bay is the most active place in the world for glacial retreat and advance and for plant-life recovery after glacial retreat. Just two hundred years earlier the bay was a thick sheet of ice that covered not only the present bay and inlets but also the entire land mass that is now at different stages of becoming reforested. The knowledge that Glacier Bay is the most reactive area in the world to glacial advance and retreat adds tremendous interest to this beautiful place. The concept of "succession"—where vegetation forms in stages after glacial retreat from lichen and moss to grasses and alder and cottonwood to "climax" forests of spruce and hemlock—is also remarkable to witness as it unfolds. The presence of wildlife, including ample numbers of the beautiful but still endangered humpback whale, makes Glacier Bay memorable and worth seeing and explains why boaters leave distant shores to visit this place.

Conclusion

There are many adventures to be had in S.E. Alaska. In future years I plan to kayak down the Stikine River from Telegraph Creek in British Columbia to Wrangell. I have plans to spend more time in Sitka and Skagway and visit more remote coves and inlets. I will be happy to hear from you about your cruising adventures.

References

Beck, Mary Giraudo. Potlatch Native Ceremony and Myth on the Northwest Coast. Seattle: Alaska Northwest Books, 1997.

Boas, Franz. Anthropology And Modern Life (1928). New York: W.W. Norton and Co.

Boas, Franz. Primitive Art (1927). New York: Dover Publications, Inc., 1955.

"British Columbia's Coast: The Canadian Inside Passage," Alaska Geographic, Volume 13, Number 3, 1986. (Anchorage, Alaska Geographic Society), Chief Editor: Robert A. Henning.

Cassidy, Frank and Norman Dale. After Native Claims? The Implications of Comprehensive Claims Settlements for Natural Resources in British Columbia. Lantsville, B.C. Oolichan Books and The Institute for Research on Public Policy, 1988.

Clearcut: The Tragedy of Industrial Forestry. Bill Devall (Ed.). Sierra Club Books, Earth Island Press, 1993.

Halliday, Jan & Gail Chehakin, in cooperation with the Affiliated Tribes of Northwest Indians. Native Peoples of the Northwest: A Traveler's Guide to Land, Art, and Culture. Seattle: Sasquatch Books, 1996.

Jung, Carl G. "Travels: The Pueblo Indians." In Memories, Dreams, and Reflections. Recorded and Edited by Aniela Jaffe. New York: Vintage Books, 1961.

John Muir: His Life and Letters and Other Writings. Terry Gifford (Ed.). Seattle: The Mountaineers, 1996.

Langdon, Steve J. The Native People of Alaska. Anchorage: Great Land Graphics, 1993.

Meggss, Geoff. Salmon: The Decline of the B.C. Fishery. Vancouver, British Columbia: Douglas & McIntyre, 1995.

Melville, Herman. Moby Dick (1851). New York: Holt, Rinehart and Winston, 1962.

Muckle, Robert J. The First Nations of British Columbia. Vancouver: UBC Press, 1998.

Native America in the Twentieth Century: An Encyclopedia. Mary B. Davis (Ed.). New York: Garland Publishing, Inc., 1996.

The Northwest Salmon Crisis: A Documentary History. Joseph Cone and Sandy Ridlington (Eds.). Corvallis: Oregon State University Press, 1996.

Prucha, Francis Paul. The Churches And The Indian Schools, 1888-1912. Lincoln: University of Nebraska Press, 1979.

Soderberg, K.A. & Jackie Durette. People of the Tongass: Alaska Forestry Under Attack. Bellevue, Washinton: The Free Enterprise Press, 1988.

Stearns, Mary Lee. Haida Culture in Custody. Seattle: University of Washington Press, 1981.

Tongass Land Management Plan Revision (six volumes). United States Forest Service. Washington D.C.: U.S. Department of Agriculture, 1997.

Treaty News: Federal Treaty Negotiation Office (March 1998 and December 1998). The Federal Treaty Negotiation Office of the Department of Indian Affairs and Northern Development represents all federal departments, agencies and the people of Canada in treaty negotiations with First Nations in British Columbia.
        PO Box 1156
        2700-650 West Georgia Strait
        Vancouver, BC V6B 4N8

Walens, Stanley. The Kwakiutl. New York: Chelsea House Publishers, 1991.

Webster, Gloria Cranmer. "From Colonization to Repatriation." In Indigena: Contemporary Native Perspectives. In Gerald McMaster and Lee-Ann Martin (Eds.), Vancouver: Douglas and McIntyre, 1992.

Wilkins, David E. Amerian Indian Sovereignty And The U.S. Supreme Court: The Masking of Justice. Austin: University of Texas Press, 1997.

Woodward, Walt. How to Cruise to Alaska (Olympia to Skagway) Without Rocking The Boat Too Much. Edmonds, Washington: Nor'westing, Inc., 1989.

Index

A

acceptable risk, vii–ix, 18

Admiralty Island National Monument (AK), 146–148

Alaska

development of, 115–117

ferries, 103

Japanese attack on, 115–116

land conservation, 117–118

Alaska National Interest Lands Conservation Act of 1980 (ANILCA), 112, 114, 117-118, 147

Alaska Native Claims Settlement Act of 1971 (ANCSA), 117-118

Alaskan State Museum, Juneau, AK, 152

Alava Bay (AK), 114–115

Alcan Highway, 115–116

Alert Bay (B.C.), 22, 77–79

American Indian Religious Freedom Act of 1978, 135–136

Amundsen, Roald, vi

Anan Creek Bear Observatory (AK), 16, 125, 137–140

ANILCA (Alaska National Interest Lands Conservation Act of 1980), 112, 114, 147

ANSCA (Alaska Native Claims Settlement Act of 1971), 117–118

Auke Bay, AK, 151–152

B

Barkley Sound (B.C.), 64

Bartlett Cove, AK, 154–156

Chatham Point (B.C.), 75
Chickamin River (AK), 31
Chief Shakes Community House, Wrangell, AK, 127–130
children on boats, 27–28, 32–33, 52
Chinese cannery laborers, 86, 88, 100
Clark, Mark, 95
Columbia River bar, 55
compass malfunctions, 56
conservationists, 116–123
costs, v–vi
crew members, 61
cruise ship travel, iv–vii, 36–37
cruising range, 44–45

D
Dall porpoises, 83
danger, 11
Davis, Jack, 89
Davis Plan, 89–90, 95, 108
Dent Rapids (B.C.), 29
Discovery Passage (B.C.), 72–73
displacement-hull boats, 39, 42–43
distance per day, 17, 26, 33, 61–62
Dixon Entrance, 15, 24, 41, 109–110
dugout canoes, vi, 93–94
duration of trips, 17, 26, 33, 34, 35, 36, 37

E
Ecklund, Dick, 83
engine hours, 17, 26, 33, 35, 36, 37
engine repairs, 43, 45
engine types, 43–44

About the Author

Leif Terdal began boating in search of salmon off the Oregon and Washington coast in the late 1960s, and was owner-operator of a commercial salmon troller during the years 1977-1991. These activities took him across the Columbia River Bar over 700 times. He remains interested in conservation efforts to preserve habitat for salmon and all wildlife. He is also the author of *Fishing Beyond The Buoys*, published by Frank Amato Press, and several books on parenting.

He retired from the Oregon Health Sciences University in 1994 after 30 years of service as a clinical psychologist. Upon his retirement, he named his new boat Second Effort, as a metaphor for this new phase of exploration.

Order Form

QTY.	Title	Price	Can. Price	Total
	Small-Boat Cruising to Alaska - Leif G. Terdal	**$15.95**	**$20.95 CN**	
	Shipping and Handling Add $3.50 for orders in the US/Add $7.50 for Global Priority			
	Sales tax (WA state residents only, add 8.6%)			
	Total enclosed			

Telephone Orders:
Call 1-800-461-1931
Have your VISA or
MasterCard ready.

INTL. Telephone Orders:
Toll free 1-877-250-5500
Have your credit card ready.

Fax Orders:
425-398-1380
Fill out this order form and fax.

Postal Orders:
Hara Publishing
P.O. Box 19732
Seattle, WA 98109

E-mail Orders:
harapub@foxinternet.net

Method of Payment:

☐   Check or Money Order

☐   **VISA**

☐   **MasterCard**

Expiration Date: _____

Card #: _____

Signature: _____

Name _____
Address _____
City _____ State ____ Zip _____
Phone (   ) _____ Fax (   ) _____

**Quantity discounts are available.
Call (425) 398-3679 for more information.
Thank you for your order!**